John L. Dudley

Tides and Tendencies of Religious Thought

John L. Dudley

Tides and Tendencies of Religious Thought

ISBN/EAN: 9783337719753

Printed in Europe, USA, Canada, Australia, Japan

Cover: Foto ©Lupo / pixelio.de

More available books at **www.hansebooks.com**

TIDES AND TENDENCIES.

Tides and Tendencies

OF

Religious Thought.

BY

J. L. DUDLEY.

Non quæras quis hoc dixerit, sed quid dicatur attende.

PHILADELPHIA:
CLAXTON, REMSEN & HAFFELFINGER,
624, 626 & 628 MARKET STREET.
1873.

TO

THE MULTITUDE OF MEN AND WOMEN
WHO, IN SILENCE AND THRALL,
ARE HUNGERING FOR MORE
BOUNTIFUL DAYS.

PREFACE.

THIS book is made up of Discourses thrown off from Sabbath to Sabbath in the ordinary course of Pulpit administration, and *Phonographically* reported for the Secular Press. The concurrent judgment and continuous demand of others, commanding the author's entire respect, have caused them to be gathered from their fugitive fortunes, and presented in a more readable and permanent form.

Literary merit is not their claim. Spoken extemporaneously before a popular audience, their free, somewhat diffuse, and almost conversational style is thence explained.

To every observing mind, *Tides and Tendencies of Religious Thought*, marked and unmistakable as they are legitimate and hopeful, constitute a leading feature of the times. Such tendencies the present volume seeks to cherish and reflect.

This Preface would be incomplete without acknowledgment of the kind offices of another, to the superintendence of whose practiced eye and hand, while the volume was passing through the press, these pages are indebted for much of their attractiveness.

J. L. D.

CONTENTS.

		PAGE
I.	*SALVATION BEFORE CHRIST*	13
II.	*THE TWO COVENANTS*	32
III.	*THE METHOD OF REVELATION*	50
IV.	*THE ONENESS OF RELIGION AND THE RACE*	71
V.	*IMITATION AND DEVELOPMENT*	85
VI.	*CHARITY*	102
VII.	*CHARACTERISTICS OF MODERN THOUGHT*	112
VIII.	*FEAR AND LOVE*	130
IX.	*THE WORTH OF THE SOUL AND ITS APPROPRIATE TREATMENT*	141
X.	*SALVATION — THE OLD AND NEW VIEW*	157
XI.	*HELP — A SUPPLEMENT, NOT A SUBSTITUTE*	171
XII.	*MAN'S NATURE DEVELOPED BY THE QUICKENING POWER OF GOD'S NATURE*	185
XIII.	*A SUFFERING CHRIST IN NORMAL ACCORD WITH NATURE AND REASON*	197
XIV.	*DOMINION OF SPIRIT OVER MATTER*	210

		PAGE
XV.	*DEBT?—OR GIFT?*	227
XVI.	*DRAWING NIGH UNTO GOD* . . .	237
XVII.	*THE LAMBHOOD OF GOD—AND HOW IT TAKES AWAY SIN*	249
XVIII.	*CHRISTIANITY AND HER FOES* . .	270
XIX.	*PERSONAL RIGHTEOUSNESS—THE RELIGION OF THE NEW TESTAMENT*	288
XX.	*A COMPARISON BETWEEN THE OLD DISPENSATION AND THE NEW* . . .	296

TIDES AND TENDENCIES

OF

RELIGIOUS THOUGHT.

I.

SALVATION BEFORE CHRIST.

> *There is no other name given under heaven whereby we must be saved.* — Acts iv. 12.

MY subject this morning is enunciated in the following proposition, namely: *The only religion that saves mankind is that which bears the Christian name.* My text is: "There is no other name given under heaven whereby we must be saved." "This is the stone which is set at naught by the builders; neither is there salvation by any other."

Salvation — saved! saved! Deeply reposing in the tranquil solitude of every human spirit is the dream, nay hope, expectation, of some final state of peace, beauty, and perfectness. Musing upon the vicissitudes of life and time, conscious of their conflict, of their tears, their ecstasy, aspiration, native and instinctive, wedded to hope equally congenial, the soul looks across the water, beyond the hills and horizons of time, to the far-off bright shore, and there expects a landing upon a new world, a beautiful world of God; a world which is to sum up all that hope holds as a reality, and faith takes in as fruition. And this has been the dream, the faith of our race; all peoples have so expected, and have indicated to themselves the great fact under various symbols. The Orientals, looking forward thus, said there was a garden, a beautiful paradise, beyond this dream-life, this winter-life of tears and suffering. The cultivated Pagan spoke of a bright Elysium, sometimes of the Isles of the blessed, as the final home of the soul. In Christian symbolism, the very same idea comes to us, as the paradise of God, the new paradise, not the old — the spiritual paradise for those who have overcome — under the figure of a city, the city of God, the beautiful city, the city of the great King. It is thought of as a new country, new realm, wherein are thrones, and principalities, and sceptres, and crowns, and honors. In a general sense, Christian thinking and Christian faith sum themselves up and ultimate in the idea of a sociality, a commonwealth, a new kingdom, as I said, the city of God; in one word, heaven. That we may bring this whole subject matter of the text more usefully upon our thought, let us aid ourselves at the outset by giving special attention to three or four particulars.

Holding the Christian idea under the symbolism of a city, the city of God, the heavenly city, I should remark, in the first place, that we think of but *one entrance* into that city, and we think correctly. There is one, but one gateway, one door, only one; and yet with this exclusiveness of entrance, lines of approach are coming from the east, and from the west, and from the north, and from the south, trailing along, pathways meeting at this very central gateway; and all the way between them are countless pathways whose converging point is this very one exclusive gateway. So that from every clime, and kindred, and nation, and tongue, from every age, from every point, these pathways come, terminating, inwardly, at the gate of entrance into the city.

The second thing I notice particularly, is the fact that comers thereto must have some *certificate* of right to enter; they must be able to give some unmistakable countersign; must have a key whose skill shall fit the ward that makes the lock that guards the one gateway to the heavenly city. And what is that key? This, exactly and exclusively: the *Christ character* in the suitor; the Christ character. Not only the Christ name, but that which is *named*, the pilgrim must possess. Having that key, he passes in, no matter where he got it. No matter whether a son of the sun, or a son of the sea; no matter whether a native of the forest, or a native of the last consummate flower of civilization and culture. Has he that key, the Christ character in his character, the pearly gate swings and he shares the inward sceptre.

Notice, in the third place, there can be no *substitute* for this key. There is no substitutional device canonized in heaven or earth, whereby a so-called saint, not a saint in character, can pick the lock of heaven. No substitute; no substitute in theory, no substitute in creed, no substitute in character. It must be personal character belonging to the suitor himself; personal, just like Christ's character.

The fourth thing to be noticed particularly here, is, that all mankind, from first to last, have had and shall have a *fair chance* in this matter. There is no poor, unfortunate culprit, so termed, created with broken limb, with monstrosity of function, with damnation written in sympathetic ink in his nature, purposely that some fire-flash might bring it to legibility. God has not created one soul in conditions of impossibility of salvation, and then damned it for not being saved. That is what I am trying to say; that is the particular thing to be noticed here. Every soul has the opportunity of being saved to the extent that God demands that he be saved; and I will show you why, presently.

Now, after this test, this sesame, certificate, key — in a word, this character by Christ Himself, there arise some very *important questions* out of the matter; and there come, streaming out of the whole of it, some inferences which the premises necessitate. To these let us now especially attend.

First, were any saved before Christ came into the world — Christ, the *only* name given under heaven whereby it is possible to be saved? Were any saved before He was named in time, before the world knew of Him, before the world heard of Him, during the long ages, the mighty centuries that waded through the night of uncertain prophecy? Any saved then? The mighty millions, the billows of generations that rolled over the sea, did any of them dash and sparkle on the bright shore? or did they all go down to the night-place? A fair question, this. We show neither our Christianity nor our manliness by blinking it, or telling the inquirer that he may not broach such a question. That is the way skeptics are made; and infidels come to scoff at the scheme of religion offered them in Christ, invoking, as they say, the contempt of their reason. Don't do it. Ask the question: Were any saved prior to about eighteen hundred years ago? Too horrible, indeed, to think of the negative answer; too terrible an impeachment of the Christian conception of the Divine attributes; too violent a logic to make any man respectable, or rather leave him respectable, even here in the dark short-sighted ways of time.

Again, if any *were* saved before Christ was heard of in this world, how were they saved? But I ought to have begun the question a little back of that. On the supposition that Christ is the only name given under heaven whereby salvation is possible, and you are pleased to suppose that some were saved before He came into the world — how were they saved? This inquiry throws us back in the next place upon the great ante-Christian economy. Assuming that men were saved before Christ, and that there is no possible salvation but in and through Christ, then you have got to have Christ back there somehow and some way. And that is what the truth is. He was there.

We are fond of calling Christianity a universal

religion; and we compliment ourselves by whetting our sharpness to the executive efficiency that detects and eliminates, not only from human nature but from the Divine nature, the elements of this universality. It is a beautiful problem; the more we work that the better. Here is a good place to take up the thought — the universality of the Christian religion. If any were saved before they ever heard of Christ, before He was ever preached to them, before any preachers were sent for that purpose, how did it happen? What was the manner and method thereof? Let us see.

There were poets before the canons of poetry. There were navigators before the art of navigation. So there were Christians before the era of Christianity. Back in old Judaism we believe that multitudes were saved; saved by the Christ, who was, and is, and is to be, the same yesterday, to-day, and forever; saved by this one grand universal Christ-scheme of human salvation, which underlay all the types and shadows, — which underflows the whole surface of time. We believe they were saved back there. Christ himself, after he had come into the world and begun to teach, said: "Search the Scriptures, for in them ye think ye have eternal life, and they are they which testify of me." Christianity was a salvation *back there*, or else Christianity is not the only religion that can save. Otherwise you are driven back upon the negative of that first horrible question, Was it possible for anybody to be saved prior to eighteen hundred years ago?

Phenomena are one thing, essence is another. Phenomena are ever changing, the transient aspect of things perishing in their using. Essences are abiding, the same yesterday, to-day, and forever. Phenomena are autumn-leaves falling every year; that which is essence is the primal vitality and force of the acorn, originally the same in the germ as in the first sprouting, and in the trunk and the arms a thousand told, throwing themselves out into the reaches of centuries. There is that which is one, unchangeable, unbroken, ever the same; and that which is changeable, coming, going, passing away. Now, is n't it about time to link ourselves with that which is permanent and everlasting, and which strikes fellowship with every truth in the world, rather than go picking up the autumn-leaves that fell from last year's growth, and last century's growth, trying to get life out of them? Is n't it better to stipulate for the heaven of prophecy, the victorious Eden at the other end, than go back and pick from the withered flowers of the primal Eden the seed of our hope? Think of it. If, now, you and I shall find ourselves able to stand up and show that Christianity has a right to this claim of universality, our ability to do so will lie along the fellowship of these universal principles which I have indicated. Our prayers must ring with the significance thereof; our sermons must be loaded with the power thereof; and our Christian characters, day by day, must show that their roots find nurture just here. It is time that Christianity be handled under methods of thought that are truly cosmopolitan, taking in not only this world, but the world which is to come. It is high time that we gear ourselves into these providential advantages which God is throwing at our feet to-day.

Having thus spoken, by the light of our thought we find ourselves instantly naming Christ backward as well as forward. He is the mighty memorial of our race, as well as its hope. Along the track of the Christ-scheme, on that scheme of religion which He names, lies all human history. Along the bright vista ahead lies all human hope, all human prophecy. Now faith finds herself able to take up the universality of Christianity and to hold it. Faith now does not hesitate; she may not comprehend by her conception exactly — that is not her business. Reason cannot do this; but faith finds herself challenged to her utmost. Here is a grandeur of function; here she wings her way to God himself, nothing short. Now, faith hath inspiration that does not flag or wither. Mystery comes pouring into it. Divinity flows in like a life river; the inspiration is as the breathing of God in such soul.

All things are the Christian's. I am the Alpha and the Omega, whispers in his faith; a grand development, a grand race-growth, a sublime unfolding system of being right out of God. This is the scheme of salvation named by Christ, than which there is no name given under heaven whereby humanity can be saved. Have all men, then, had a chance to be saved? Is there any exclusiveness or respect of persons or opinions by God? Did not this scheme of salvation begin before time? Isn't it throbbing through all time? Will it not last on beyond time, this one grand method and power of salvation named by the Christ-God? O how broad! how broad!

O, suitor at the shining gate, it will not be asked what tribe you belonged to on earth; what nation, what kindred, what clime, what people. It will not be asked what religion you belonged to — that never will be thought of. It will not be asked whether you are all Puritans or all Papists; whether you are Calvinists or Arminians; Universalists or Quakers; Presbyterians, Episcopalians, Swedenborgians, or even — Congregationalists. That won't be asked. No time for that — no opportunity for such waste of heavenly thought. Autumn-leaves, all those; good in their season and for their use, but done with now. What is the fruit? Have you this key, this character? Don't present your substitute; don't present your creed; don't borrow anybody's opinions; don't get the advantage of anybody's reputation. What are *you*, O soul? Show your mark — yes, your character.

I am in transport, I confess, at the grand thought of this Divine and sympathetic unfolding of God's love, wisdom, and power, on our nature and our race! Here we are but little germs of being; but little seminal potencies unstarted. The transporting thought is, that I was created into this sympathetic environment of God which spans the ages; whose heart, throbbing hither and thither, is bounded only by the boundary of eternity. I am blooming a little to-day beneath this all ensphering summer of God, sings the soul. I am starting immortal generations beneath the favoring touch of this Divine sympathetic provision. And then I am kept on by way of transplantation into the upper garden, "where angels walk and seraphs are the wardens." It is transporting! I thank God to-day for life, for being. The harps we hear of, the palms that shall wave, and the crowns that glitter, are only faint and feeble symbols of the gushing music that shall well up from within; of the grand prerogatives that will be mine and yours if we answer to the Divine call so coming to us; and all things shall be but a stringed instrument of glory that will sing forever and ever at our inspiring touch. I am moved to ecstasy when I think of man's nature, thus held in the warm, sympathetic environment of God; and am chilled to frost at the thought of repelling and rejecting all that, and dreaming of it after all opportunities are lost!

If you would feel the power of Christianity, come down into the arterial circulation where the blood flows, coming directly warm from the heart. Don't live up among the blue veins which have distributed their nurture once, and are going back to get a new supply. Go down to the universal, perpetual, vital elements of nature and religion. O how we belittle Christianity by doing anything else! How we belittle ourselves, and shrink and wither by feeding, not upon the substance, not upon the enduring, but upon some mere passing phenomena, some floating rumors of the ages, what some hundreds of men voted five hundred years ago, or what somebody said or told us of! How we become self-belittled thus, and our very thinking chatters with chills and rattles like the bones of the dead. Christ is the God named through man. The Christ-power is the God-power unto salvation.

Out of Paganism it was also possible for souls to be saved. They could be plucked from it as brands from the burning. I said, in noticing my fourth introductory particular, that all mankind have, and must have had, a chance for salvation, or the honor of God is in question. Pagans, therefore, must have had a chance. And moreover, if Revelation in the New Testament be true after it is made, certainly they had; for Paul tells us that they were without excuse, not only for not worshipping God, but for not worshipping his eternal power and Godhead. Godhead — what is meant by that? It means the Father, means the Son, means the Holy Ghost. Now Paganism is nothing but the benighted, feeble striving of man's religious nature to get at its answer; the native hunger of his humanity striving to get bread somehow and somewhere. If it were possible for that hunger to become conscious, the counterpossibility was, as it is, the bread of life available. Don't you know how in the old Prophets it reads: "The Desire of all nations." That is the theme of one of the grandest courses of the Hulsean lectures, given by Dean Trench several years ago in England, — Christ, the Desire of all Nations. Now if that desire were there subjectively, how are you going to handle the consistency of Heaven, putting it there with no possibility of getting at the true object of the desire? It cannot be done. Missionaries are full of testimony that Pagans not unfrequently have subjectively the Christ state. Now the objective answer to that was indicated by Paul. This Christ system, which is the God system, or the way of God's coming into us, or the way of God's manifesting himself to us, has always been in exact providential *adaptation* to the time, condition, and manner of the race. Yes, it is possible for Pagans to be saved, or God would not hold them guilty for not being saved.

I add that even under the primal condition of nature is salvation possible. Such teachings have the flaming heavens rendered declaring the glory of God; such teachings have the lessons of the lilies and the flowers of the field rendered. It is *possible* for man to be saved under the lessons of God's natural world. We don't look at this; and because we don't think it, fail to believe it. Why, to quote Paul again, his affirmation in Romans is exactly to the point; things that are made being seen from the creation of the world, sufficiently reveal God; so that men are without excuse for not knowing Him and worshipping Him, even His eternal power and Godhead; which knowledge and worship bring salvation. We forget sometimes how beautifully the new Book reads: "*By* Him and *for* Him are all things made that are made." He who names the only scheme of salvation has his own sign-manual in these flowers. By Him and for Him — there is a great logic in nature, strung together by the Christ-God. It shakes hands with the logic of Providence, strung together by the Christ-God. And they twain are one with the logic of the Book, strung together by the Christ-God. But all this which Christ has joined together, your scepticism and atheism and infidelity, and mine, may not put asunder. Therefore we say that this view of Him who names the only scheme of salvation, makes salvation *possible* in all conditions of humanity, in all races, under all religions; the possibility lying exactly here in the fact that God himself, the Christ-God, as to the matter in hand, is always so *adapted* to human want as to be available, and to take away all excuses from that humanity, if the proffered boon be not accepted. The possibility lies, let me repeat, in the fact that salvation is ever available from the providential adaptation of Jesus Christ to the wants of the human soul.

Passing this, I remark again that we find, under such views, Jesus Christ very much broader than we sometimes suppose; the Christian religion which He names, very much ampler than the two covers, not of this Book, but some books; the possibilities of salvation sweeping a vaster scale than the stretch and the soar and the diving of some men's minds would seem to indicate. In a word, infinitely broad, if we dare to be consistent — broad as God Himself, whose thought and whose heart this scheme of love and mercy is. When we come to take up the matter intelligently, thinking about it as men can think and ought to think, we find that this is the underlying scheme of Providence. We find that God has but one grand scheme of relations toward man, starting from eternity, unfolding all through time, unbroken, unbroken, until the consummation in the world of eternity at the other end; born of God, under the conduct of God, maturing in God at last, from whom and through whom and to whom are all things.

We recollect a sermon two or three Sundays ago on the coming One, the memorial Name which shall be "my name forever," the name of the Comer. Here it is. Christianity has been coming into the world, into human life, into human character, so fast and far as man himself would permit it, ever since men began to exist. It is the unfolding of the scroll; it is the development of the drama; it is the growth of the grand system of Divine life propagating itself here in our human life, and no scheme of self-constituted human tinkers to patch up a poor administration of the Divine government. God from beginning, God all through, and God at last. "I am the Alpha and Omega," says this very name, Christ, — "the first and the last;" the golden chain whose primal link is a primeval heart-throb of the everlasting Jehovah, and whose terminal one — the chain having circled the universe — joins back to its mate in the beginning; broader, broader vastly, than He is sometimes thought.

But passing on, I notice, in the next place, that just here it is that we strike the elements of *universality* in Christianity. We are fond of calling it the religion of the world, the race. We sometimes pray for its diffusion. We sometimes think we are heart-heavy because of the mighty millions given to destruction from the lack of it. All well; but let us be intelligent with ourselves. What are the elements of universality? Wherein lie the fitness and substance of this all-inclusive characteristic? If we will look, — if we had time right here, we could come upon that. Has not Christ been the same yesterday, to-day, and forever? That which in Him is the same yesterday, to-day, and forever, makes Him universal as the Saviour. That in Christianity and its grand system of thought and inspiration, which makes it the same yesterday, to-day, and forever, constitutes the elements of universality in it, fit for all time, all places, all conditions of man — starting from God, coming to God again. The countertruth to that is this, namely: that in man's nature which makes him a fit subject for what is universal in Christ and his religion, is the element of universality in man, exactly. That which is the same yesterday, to-day, and forever in man, is the universality of the race, what is common to it. Naming it anywhere, if we do not put a false name, we hit what is in every man. Exactly the same in all men of all times, of all climes, of all races, in all conditions — exactly the same, made the same. Put that and the everlasting Christ together, and as one is hunger and the other is bread, you have consummated the grand reality of salvation stipulated for from the foundation of the world.

I might delay at length upon this. You see I am tempted to. You perceive I ought to do it, in order to clear up the whole matter; but you give me not the hours to do it now. I should thus be obliged to note the grand native impulses planted in man's soul by God. I should be obliged to examine the original intuitions of his nature which God deposited there as the postulate of the argument that should link the human soul to his existence, and the conscious affirmation of that existence. I should be thrown back upon the constituent elements of our being: and when I had brought them forth, and awakened them to their true function, then I could show Jesus Christ and His religion, and you would see how the two fit. Thus we should understand in what consists the universality of this religion, so Divine and so human, throbbing and thrilling through the history of the whole race from everlasting to everlasting, as God's grand scheme of salvation.

But having said so much, I pass on to ask, Isn't it about time in the world, after eighteen hundred years, nay, after four thousand years, nay, more, after countless ages, as science begins to tell us, through which this Christ drama has been hinting and whispering and struggling itself forth into manifestation — isn't it about time to begin to handle the great question under these broad elementary constituencies that enter into its substance? Is n't it about time to drop a great deal of the sacred "putter" that is made the sum and substance upon which men have staked their salvation, and begin to take up these elements of universality, the great conception and scheme of God in Jesus Christ, and His religion towards man?—to take them up in the length and breadth and abiding persistency of their very nature? If Christ is thus broad, if all the things are true which we specified in our introduction, is n't it about time for the intelligence of the world, for the manhood of the world, to welcome gladly these elements of the problem, and make them the bone and marrow of pulpit-handling and pew-handling? Is n't it time, in a word,—since God has struck the hour for it, opened the way, and unrolled the scroll of his thought sufficiently,—to take up the universal elements in this problem as they challenge the reason of man, that feature in the Divine likeness, than which none is grander, diviner, or more significant? Is n't it better to be following after these lengthening cords, and holding on to those fixed firm stakes of universality, than it is to be praying solemn prayers on one side of the mouth, and making up faces at rationalism on the other side? No man in that way can serve two masters. The time is at hand when all these elements of universality must be marshalled and disciplined like an army drilled, and all through Christendom, and all through the world, they must come together as a solid host to breast the assaults that are made against

Christianity. You cannot tie up the old thrums and rotten strings that did baby-work once — a good Divine work, because that was the way God adapted himself to the world at that time. You are to have the strong cords and the long cords — immortally long and divinely strong — of universality as they touch Christ and his religion and providence, and as they touch you, your nature, which that religion is for.

Christianity is no thing of modern birth, ending in apparent death. It is older than time, continuing on beyond time, born out of God and his eternity, trailing on the path of immortality. And I shall live and think and unfold the scroll hereafter; yea, not only as I could here, but infinitely better. So there comes the gentle, tearful refrain, "I would not live always." The heart liveth forever. Mightily more, yonder, shall be the revelation of this one Christ scheme towards us, than we can get here. Here it just germinates in our conception. There it shall bloom and sing in the great cantos of reason and rhapsody, and there shall be no flagging to the tide of that song.

One said I shall be satisfied when I awake in Thy likeness. The likeness of Christ and God sleeps in every soul, in capacity. The problem of salvation is to fill those capacities with the substance of the very God himself.

See to it, then, not only that you bear the name of the saving One and Power, but that you bear what the name means. When you think of the

Central City, when you think of the one gate, when you think of the multitude of paths that converge there, remember one thing: the *key*, nothing but the key — only that. Have you the nature, as well as the name, the " I am " — who named the only power in the universe according to Christianity, by which man can be saved? Have you this key? Seeking that, having it, hold no anxiety in your soul's outlook, as it gazes toward the land beyond the great sea.

II.

THE TWO COVENANTS.

The mediator of the new covenant. —
Hebrews xii. 24.

INTIMATELY interwoven with the thought and associations of all Christendom, is the idea of two *covenants*, called the Old and the New; sometimes called the "*covenant of works*" and the "*covenant of grace.*"

The old covenant, or the covenant of works, so called, is held in this fashion: It is believed that God made a contract, or covenant, or agreement, or whatever word may best carry the idea, with Adam, the first man of the race, as its head and representative, to the effect that, should he keep the command, observe the prohibition, and successfully carry himself through the proposed order and trial, he should live, he should be saved; and therein and thereby all his posterity, the race of men, should live and be saved and not die.

The test pivoted on a single prohibition. In the phrasing of the Book: "*Of every fruit of the garden might this first man eat save one; of the fruit of the tree of knowledge of good and evil he might not eat.*" To partake of it was to die. And in that death, and in that failure of Adam's trial, were involved the death and destruction of all his posterity. That was the first covenant, or the covenant of works, based upon this primal Edenic transaction.

The problem, you remember, failed. The first man stood not in his integrity, but came to disaster. And consequently, the idea is, all mankind are involved in that disaster. That act in the drama is closed. That dispensation of works is ended. That first covenant is exploded, and there is nothing more in time or human life about it but the mere record of its nullity.

After that failure, a new proposition was made by God; a new covenant was made called the covenant of grace, or Christ. This was to take the place of the old one; to be a substitute where it had failed; a necessity created by that very failure; necessitated by this disaster and doom and death connected with the first covenant. This new covenant so called, substituted for the old one which had been broken and had failed, is also called Christianity or the Gospel, the covenant of Christ, the hope of the world. Now, the faith of the world pivots on this instead of the other.

So it seems that if Adam had only shown a little firmness, had only stood his ground under the assault of temptation, and done what he should have done, and what he could have done if he was to blame for not doing it, then this new covenant had never had any necessity, or place, or fitness of any kind, in the fortunes of the human race. Had Adam done what he ought to have done, he would have defeated this latter order and dispensation of the Gospel, by having superseded the necessity of it; by having made the very idea of it futile, inasmuch as there would have been no need of it.

Now I leave it to you to manage the problem — for I decline the responsibility — how it is that infinite Wisdom came into such a pass of things, that if Adam had done what he ought to have done, and thus had pleased God, the whole Gospel dispensation would have been superseded and we never should have heard of Christ. Life and immortality had never been brought to light. A new nature had never been dreamed of, and all that prophetic vista of glory and grandeur which the unsealed vision of man now drinks in by the clarifying touch of the Gospel, had been as night, as nothing, never having come so much as into the dream of human anticipation. Had Adam pleased God at first, he would have wiped out the second Adam in advance, and all the grandeur and glory resulting therefrom. You must manage that for yourselves. Such is the putting and position of matters.

That I speak not at random when I say that the general belief and acknowledged faith of Protestant Christendom with regard to the two covenants — the one substituted for the other, and the necessity of the second created by the failure of the first — is as above stated, is obvious. For, on this very point, that celebrated document, the Westminster Confession or Catechism, speaks directly, sustaining exactly this view.

The 12th article of that Confession reads thus:

"When God had created man he entered into a *covenant* of life with him, upon condition of perfect obedience, forbidding him to eat of the tree of knowledge of good and evil, upon the pain and penalty of death." The 16th article reads thus: "A *covenant* being made with Adam, not only for himself but for his posterity, all mankind sinned in him and fell with him." The 15th article is on this wise: "The sin whereby our first parents fell was their *eating the forbidden fruit.*" And then comes in the 20th article: "God, of his own good pleasure, did enter into a *covenant* with Christ to deliver man out of a state of sin and misery, and bring him into salvation by a Redeemer."

This is standard authority, and is the same thing that we just presented. The whole grounds on the *Edenic transaction.*

It is assumed, you perceive, that *before the fall no covenant of grace was needed.* God was running the world very much on the system that men sometimes call Deism — the system that recognizes God, indeed, out of sight, but no revelation of Himself in any distinct or set form. This assumption carries the idea that there was no Christianity, no Gospel, no Christ, no *new covenant*, prior to the failure of the Edenic transaction, which necessitated Christ and the Gospel and the covenant of grace. It assumes that the antagonism between the new and the old was exactly between the covenant of works made with Adam in Eden, and that made in and with Christ *after* the failure of that first arrangement.

So that, upon each, three or four things need to be noticed particularly.

First: You will observe that the New Testament nowhere, from first to last, refers to that Edenic transaction as a *covenant of works*, in opposition to the Gospel or the *covenant of grace*. The reference by the New Testament is to the *Mosaic* order of things, to the Sinaitic code, to the whole economy of Jewish life and nationality and polity, extant prior to the advent of Christ. The *contrast* between the new and the old, is between *Christ* and *Moses*, and not between Christ and Adam. Read the New Testament and you will find it so. And on that ground Paul's reasoning stands firm, whether in Hebrews or Galatians, in Colossians, Corinthians, Romans, or other epistles. He tried to lift Jewish faith and life from the old adjustment, namely, the ceremonial, into the new as enunciated in Christ. That is the whole push and pull of the argument of Paul in these grand epistles. He would have them take the new in Christ, instead of the old in Moses, or Israel, or David, replacing the whole Jewish nationality, theocracy, monarchy, polity, and all. They wax old, but this is the same yesterday, to-day, and forever.

Mighty hints of logic in these casual words, whose latent fire, by implication, consumes all the cobwebs and rubbish that have tangled the minds of men from the beginning until now.

Secondly: The real truth about the new covenant, or the covenant of grace, is exactly this: *It was or-*

dained, in the *Christ of God, from the foundation of the world.* It is that covenant which unfoldeth the eternal purpose of God that was hidden beneath the ages as a mystery so long, and which, in the latter days, and in the fulness of time, came out into manifestation to the world. The *covenant of grace* was the *original* covenant; not made after the failure of the Edenic transaction, but existing prior to its inauguration; existing prior to the creation of man; in the great language of the inspired epistles, ordained from the foundation of the world, in the beginning, from the old eternity.

The third thing to notice is that the Edenic transaction itself, instead of being in antagonism to this original covenant of grace, is *concurrent therewith;* instead of militating against it, is necessarily expository thereof. The truth is, that early transaction is a part of the great connected whole; one link in the unbroken chain of the development of God, ordained in the Christhood of God, from the beginning of the infinite nature. So that Adam and Abraham, and the whole Davidic line, to the grand and mournful catastrophe of the Jewish polity, are so many links of that unbroken chain; so many acts on the stage of time, one after another, through which the one original drama of the grace covenant is evolved and brought forward.

In the fourth place, notice why, the truth being thus, this eternal covenant is called the "*new covenant.*" It is, in fact, older than all others. Why call it the new one? For the same reason that any *news* is called new. The good news which the angels proclaimed was old as eternity, but *new in time;* not heard of before; a novelty freshly divulged; a secret just become patent. God has spoken what He thought in silence from all eternity, and that is the news; never heard of in time before. This is the revelation of the mystery hidden beneath the ages, of Ephesians and Colossians, called new for the above reason; new in the order of time; old in the order of things.

Come now to notice, more particularly, the idea and meaning of the word covenant itself. This covenant that God made, was it of the nature of a contract, after all? of a bargain? of an agreement? It takes two parties for that; and in all such cases each party has its right, has its option. Either party is competent to suggest, consent, concur, withdraw, or object. Each party is voluntarily bound. There is no compulsion about it. There can be no right or validity in a contract where tyranny imposes it; it is despotism, it is wrongness; it is not a covenant.

The idea of covenant in the text, if not this — and I submit that it is not, and cannot be such; God did not offer it as a party to a commercial transaction with Adam or the world — if not this, I say, what then? I reply it was the divine offer, the divine plan, the divine scheme propounded by God himself alone with relation to man, unfolding his wisdom in that relation, setting forth his love in that relation, and also his power. It was the grand scheme which God threw at the feet of man, holding in itself what

He proposed to do *for* man, and *how* He proposed to exalt him and perfect him, and make him a child of the new world; to make him eligible to a peerage in his new and spiritual dominion. This is the mighty plan. I am thy Father; I am thy protector; I am thy provider; says God. This is what I propose to do for you, and in you, and through you. The contract was made *with Himself;* it was his own *voluntary* proposition, without consultation aside from Himself; God's offer, God's plan of making man what He would have man to be.

Having thus spoken of the covenants in their relation to each other, and as to their grounds, let us now take up the idea of *Mediator*— Jesus the "Mediator of the new covenant." What does this mean? What idea does the word convey? It is almost inextricably interwoven with the thought and association of Christendom, that the Mediator of the New Testament is one *standing between two belligerent parties*, having in hand the great matter of their quarrel,— his mediatorship being exclusively to secure peace, negotiate a reconciliation. The mediatorship of Christ is limited to that, and Christendom predicates nothing else of its function. But is this correct? What does this word mean? What is the idea conveyed? Forget, if you can, all historic associations; drop all the glasses through which you have looked at the word, and come at once to its meaning. What is it?

When the Government of the United States sends a plenipotentiary to England, or Berlin, or Vienna, does that mean, necessarily, that the two nations are at war? and that the high official had not been sent save as there had been this hostile condition of things? We send ministers in times of peace, do we not? And there are thousands and thousands of interests to be handled by that mediatorship, that have nothing to do with quarrels. A merchant sends his agent throughout the land; does that imply that the commercial interests of the country are in civil strife, and all this agent has to do is to make peace and reconciliation? And unless it is so, does it follow that the word negotiator, or mediatorship, has no meaning? Does it follow that the landlord and his tenant on noble acres, are in a deadly feud simply because the former sends his factor to collect rents of the latter? They may be lifelong and loving friends, and the factor have nothing to do but with their friendship. Does it follow that every shopkeeper in Milwaukee is simply a pacific negotiator between the consumer and the producer, because there is a quarrel between them? Are father and children at variance, because he employs a tutor to teach and correct them? There may indeed be conflicting interests in all the relations supposed; there may be hostilities; these may be deadly in their alienations, or they may not. It is not necessary that the condition be a hostile one in order that we come to the idea of *mediator*.

Christ was an *internuncius*, an official, a functionary, I submit, between the *heart of God and his children*. In the first place you see at a mere glance, if you are reflecting men or women, how impossible it is for the Absolute and Infinite to hold any intercourse with the finite, except through a medium, or by mediatorship. You see at once it is not necessary to assume a *quarrel* between God the Father and his children. Why, Himself is the grand mediator after all. He mediates between the hunger and bread of every child — the grand commissary, or mediatorial provider, not for wrath or hate's sake, but for love's sake. You see that this office was not ordained *lately*, but was ancient as God; was included in his purpose and beneficence from the foundation of the world. Indeed, it was the very matter of the original covenant of grace, and there *never was any other covenant of grace*. We were created into it. The stars awoke their bright beholding in the arms of it, and all creation, and all things that are made in any way are made in the interest of it; and without the interest of this mediatorship nothing is made that is made You see that it never has been superseded — never. *It is the original policy of the original government of God, laid down when He ordained it.* You perceive that this line of purpose has *never been departed from, from first to last.* Every time the curtain has been lifted of the theatre of Providence, in eternity or time, it has disclosed some new act of this unbroken line of mediatorship. God is executing that purpose now. It was enunciated by Christ more grandly than by any other man. It was whispered in the promise of Eden; it was typified in the figure of Noah; it was divulged in the transaction with Abraham; it was adumbrated beneath all the types and shadows of Judaism; till at last it came forth in full articulate utterance in the sublime Word — God manifest in the flesh. The grand *Logos* of the Alexandrian was taken up by John to speak forth this grander continuity of the heavenly manifestations. Here you have the seed-thought of the Lord, or Immanuel, "God with us," down here in the low *intermediate* state between the Infinite and the finite; between the Absolute and the relative; between God and man; here working to work man up from his low primal state, to the high consummate finish of the hereafter.

Now, do we not know that nothing is more difficult than for men to *broaden* and *lengthen* and *deepen* their ideas of things? And it is more difficult in religion than anything else, because there is a sort of sacred bias, a sort of conscientious thrall about it. But from stage to stage, life must broaden its thinking, must expand its ideas; and it must be able to leave the old stations and emigrate out of them into new worlds of light and glory, or the world will die. Confine the bird inside the shell because it began there, and the thing will die. Imprison the callow brood in the primitive nest, and it will never have wing-power, but will die. You must emigrate, however sacred may be the cradle in which you were first rocked. You must leave the old places where your faith was first warmed to bud and bloom, and the very bloom itself must *fall off*, or no fruit will set.

We know how averse men are in their Christian thinking, to any *revision* of their ideas. I don't expect to dislodge from your minds this morning — I shall scarcely begin to — the old set and stereotyped idea of two covenants, one to make up for the deficiencies of the other; as if one half of the exchequer of God at last had to be expended to repair some trouble that He had not foresight to provide for in the beginning. I don't expect to dislodge this; and I will add that it may not be wisest, voluntarily, even to open the eyes suddenly to the sun, bright and beauteous as it is. Nature herself has taught us lessons here. Out of midnight, gentle dawn comes with gentle, velvet fingers, to touch the eyelids and gradually fret the organ of vision into confidence enough to awake and behold the light and live. We could not see God and live, we are told. We may be injured by the violence of a sudden flash of truth, some of us not having looked that way or gotten the habit of it. Men don't want to re-examine their faith. They don't want the trouble of it. They are conscientious a great many times; they think it was once right, and what is once right is always right. Ah! Is it? Once an egg always an egg? Once a mud-hut always a mud-hut? Because that was the first habitation of civilization, must it always be? We must re-examine our faith or die. Old Judaism said she would not re-examine; and she stuck to the promise until about ten or fifteen years ago, and so she was a vagabond in the world. Old priestcraft and old priest-ridden Europe said they would not re-examine their faith. When Luther sounded his trumpet-blast, the infallible Mother held on to the unrevised; and now her gouty feet and clumsy legs, like a fugitive, are seeking some shelter and rest for her last waning days.

O, those noble Bereans! How much better than most of us, who examined even the word of God itself! and they did it daily, to see "whether these things were so." Who have examined these two covenants to see whether they are so? But they are not the Word of God; they are but the sayings of men.

What would you think of a man who should say, "I prefer to take passage on a ship constructed by some former generation; I prefer to cross the Atlantic in that, rather than risk your new ones." What would you think of it? Why there is not a ship, however staunchly built, sailing out of New York harbor, that is not subject to re-examination every time she casts off for a new voyage. If this were not so, would you be underwriter? Would you be consigner to any such custody as that? Would you be passenger? The children of this world are wiser than the so-called children of light. All the underwriters in the world could not make strong the worm-eaten and rotten keel and ribs and sheathing of a craft built sixteen generations ago. It was sound as God's thought then; constructed by the best skill on earth then; navigated by the latest and most approved charts. But would you think of consigning a cargo to Liverpool, one of you — or any other man with his eyes open — if you knew that the ship would be navigated by a chart a thousand years old?

In your faith you are shipping not only for England but for eternity; not only a few paltry dollars' worth, but the worth of your soul, in a craft that you *refuse even to re-examine*. Are you and I to stand up and challenge the faith of the whole world, or endorse a policy which says, "Unless you give your faith to what was laid down in past ages of the world, I will confiscate your property, I will stretch you upon inquisitorial racks, I will hand you over to the fagot?" Are we ready to do that, and yet refuse an examination of our propositions? It is no sign of an intelligent Christian to do this; and thousands upon thousands would sooner go down in the old craft, where they are comfortably nested in their berth, than take the trouble to reship. Not that they would put it in that way, but that is what it is.

The Westminster divines, from whom I have quoted, met in 1648 — in the 17th century. They were appointed as a commission by the Parliament, not by God, or God's spirit, or any college of apostles, but by the civil power, without inspiration or infallibility, to get together some sort of codification to compose the distracted thought of the time. They met. They were good pious men; good men as ever lived before them; good men as have lived since. They did their work as well as they could. And yet that assembly was divided. There were hot discussions, and the things that they carried were carried by a mere majority, with strong protest against them. And yet what they did, has constituted the Protestant spectacles through which the Bible has been looked at ever since. It is by their refracting power that the unity of God has been resolved into this double covenant; and the view has been perpetuated. Those divines were not God's infallible agents, but the agents of the Parliament of Great Britain.

During the session of the late Œcumenical Council at Rome, we laughed to scorn the idea of infallibility voted upon a mortal by an assembly of mortals as imperfect as himself; and even at that, so divided that their vote was carried against a very strong minority. We remember how the most intelligent Bishops in that convention were opposed to that barefaced dogma. The brain of Germany was opposed to it, just as the heart of France favored it. And yet we stand here to-day, voting infallibility to the British Parliament of two hundred years ago, where they had no better agreement in their Council than there was at Rome the other day. Men had rather be let alone, a great many times, than take the trouble to be made better. They had rather have ease, and comfort, and spontaneous rest, than to take the trouble and responsibility, and industry enough, to be better. They will accept anything, many times, rather than be at the trouble of doing anything that looks like improvement, or of doing and being anything different.

The truth is, God from the very beginning of creation, and as far back as we can go in our conception, beyond creation, has been translating and manifesting Himself. The first rough draught was thrown off in creation itself, in symbols, in signs, in flashing glories, and mystic hieroglyphics; and the world could hardly decipher them. It looked and saw men and God in the fantastic dream of waking. The dream was sometimes of glory and sometimes of gloom. Even then, in the darkness, there was a skilful mixing of color that was going to paint daylight on the coming sky.

Then again God threw out a better translation of Himself in the making of man. And all along through providence, He has dropped the curtain and translated, and then lifted it and thrown out the translation to be studied and read of men; and so from symbol into figure, and from figure into event, He has come; until at last He spoke articulate in his own Word made flesh, and the world knew Him. And now if we don't read even while running—nay, though fools, it is because we love darkness rather than light.

God is not done yet. Finer and more literal translations of Himself are to be rendered in coming time. As long as our race shall live, God will have something more to give out; and it will be all in the line of this original, unbroken purpose, which is the covenant of grace.

Have no misgivings, therefore, friends; no misgiving as to faith, as to truth. Stand to the covenant which says, "Before Abraham was I am." Wonderful allies are coming out of the darkness into light, and offering their enlistment in this work of faith. Let us not tarry around the old tents, the old camp-fires. Strike the tents, and let the camp-fires wane; and advance, for God is our Leader.

Men have failed in all ages and under all religions, and will continue to fail. Every man is an Adam over again; not because Adam was his master, but because he is a man.

Whenever, O soul, you sit in disaster — sit in tears; whenever you feel broken with the weight of things, understand you are sitting at the feet of wisdom. Failures are teachers; and by the light of their wisdom you re-illumine your torch. There is no haphazard in the covenant plan; it is straight and connected. We feel, indeed, that we are disimparadised at first. But every mortal is thus set into a new path, whose everlasting paradise is at the other end.

The Fathers gave you and me faith founded on cloister life; but we must get out of that into the broad live world, where the heart tugs and toils; where patience kindles the fires of virtue; where character is crowned or discrowned, and the new manhood gets its rough hewing. The broad world of living humanity is the theatre of Christly development. Thither go forth, says God the Father, and achieve. There build your great convictions; there make the true confession. In life is Immanuel, the same yesterday, to-day, and forever.

Do you not know that the newest things are always the oldest? Do you not know that the first is always the last? The eternal covenant there is called new, because it was the old one not heard of before. Time is but the manifestation of eternity.

When the reaper shall put his sickle into the last harvest, it will be to gather the fruitage of the first planting. When we shall be in the blaze and bloom of Paradise above, that Paradise will be but the executed covenant ordained from the foundation of the world.

Accept, then, this bond of unbroken continuity, this linked chain of grace and purpose from first to last. Grasp this unity of faith and knowledge of the Son of God, and so keep the original covenant of life. It is one and full, spanning the ages, covering all human vicissitude, threading together all finite phenomena, till the last link in time joins on to the first in eternity. Write this ONE covenant in your faith; make it the law of your life, and execute it in your CHARACTER; then, nor life, nor death, nor temptation, nor disaster, shall separate you from the Love that ordained it from the beginning.

III.

THE METHOD OF REVELATION.

He that built all things is God. — Heb. iii. 4
For He was before all things. — Col. i. 17.

SO there was gravitation before apples fell or orchards grew. There was electricity before there were thunderbolts or telegraphs. There was art long anterior to artists; religion long before there were any saints or sinners. Before Abraham was, Christ is; and prior to all revelations He was and is God forever.

Last Sunday, by a rearward course of thought, we followed back Christianity from scattered hints to a connected whole, founded in the nature of things, even in God Himself. This morning, by a reverse order of thought, we wish to begin with God, and follow Him out and forward, along the ways of self-manifestation, unfolding, or revelation. Then, we went from the branches back to the root; now, we would begin at the root and work toward the branches. Then, we passed from the finite to the Infinite; now, we would go from the Infinite to the finite. At that time we went up from diversity into unity; to-day we would go down from unity into diversity. Last Sabbath we felt our way back from man to God; to-day we would feel our way from God to man.

And here you must let me *assume* the existence of God without proving it; for your patience would find fault with me for two things if I should attempt the proof. First, for mixing up matters that should be kept separate in the handling; and secondly, for taxing you for long hours beyond the terms of all stipulation. So the validation of the existence of God in the human mind, will give us opportunity for another discourse. God, then, exists. Coiled up in Him, if we may use such human language, lies all that ever did or will come out of Him. Enfolded in God lay the universe, providence, and redemption, as an oak lies folded in an acorn—the germ; that is, order, intelligence, purpose, love, as they stand stated in all these external expressions, inhere in God, natively. The grand scheme into which those few hints last Sunday guided us, validated ultimately in the nature of things—the nature of God Himself—slept in his being from eternity.

The final scheme, I say. Now, from that point let us think a little outward, saying everything that can be said in forty-five minutes—or sixty, if accidentally I should touch the latter. Beginning at the God point, let us think toward time and man.

The first conception that we have of the manifestation of God, or the revelation of Him, comes from *Creation*. His works—Nature, the declarative glory of the heavens, the mute, mystic ciphers in the deep earth, are the works of God as much as this Book. Everything that God has manifested of his own thought, love, and will, is revelation thus far and therein.

The next conception after creation, that we have of the manifestation of God, is in law, government, rule; or, in one word, *history*—or Providence, if you like it better. For there we perceive not only intelligence, not only order, not only the enunciation of some previous design, but we behold a grand connected course of things. It is a chain with no lacking links. History, as men have come to understand it, and accept it, and handle it, is a growth from some primal conception vital through the ages, through the race, on to the end of the race, out of sight. That is another revelation, another grand book, as really as this Book is a revelation; not specifically the same thing, but in the same unbroken interest.

The next conception we have of this unfolding of God's purposes, thoughts and designs, we get in *man* himself—in his nature, his soul. Here we come to the dim outline of the original as we get it nowhere else. Here we touch the personal manifestation of God. Here revelations begin to be *conscious*. Old nature is not conscious; man *is* conscious—outlining the Maker and the Father dimly in prophecy, in history. When we come to the end of this matter of man, the design as in him, the purpose for which he was created as a manifestation or revelation of God, it will be just as if a man should look into a looking-glass; or rather as if God himself had at last burnished a bright plate that would glance back his own face. So that here we pick up the grand old ideas of Providence, of creation, of redemption. These three are one, just as the links in a chain make one. They are one in origin, one in end, one in administration — one revelation of God.

There are two great determining instincts in the world — call them institutions if you like it better, any name that will mean the thing best to you. But we say here, there are two great determining instincts animating the world: one is the instinct of *self;* the other is the instinct of something *higher than self,* outside of self and beyond. One is you, is me; the other is God. These are not deductions; they are not inductions; they are self-affirmative; they are perpetually emphasizing self-assertions. The first selfhood, or self-consciousness, roots in the second, or in God. The second, or the instinct of God himself, is manifested in the first. You root in the Divine nature; the Divine nature blossoms in you. These two reciprocal vitalities, these two great primal, correlate functions, make creation, make history, make redemption. Creation, providence, redemption, get their interpreting key-thought out of these two instincts.

Now, it is to be observed, in noticing the law of revelation and manifestation of God, in the first place, that all early conceptions of religion by the human race — all early manifestations of God or revelations to the world, are *metaphorical,* not logical after the fashion of modern sermons; but metaphorical, symbolical, highly figurative, emblematic, parabolic; great pictures adapted exactly, you perceive, to the early and crude state of our race — that is, its childhood state.

What do you do, parents, with your children the first years of their lives? Do you not give them playthings, play with them, talk high wisdom in the language of nonsense, forge and fashion and link syllogisms in terms of beautiful illusions? Don't you suppose God is as wise as you are? By and by, when they become men, they will not go back to their playthings to complete the superstructure of their manhood. You go back there for the instinct that prophesied your coming; and if you find that, it will be a clue to the divine wisdom that ordained it, as well as to yourself.

In the second place, it is a law of revelation to go *higher and higher*, each manifestation of God being in advance of the preceding one. After nature, history; after history, humanity. Or, to handle our thought on the form of historic religions, first, Fetichism; the lowest kind of religion — a religion that makes a god of a stick or a worm, calling it Him, a Being, a Power. After that, Polytheism; a higher range of thought, a broader, truer conception; for while there be many gods under this, the idea of Divinity is very different in Polytheism from what it is in Fetichism. After Polytheism, Monotheism. Here the mind gathers out of broken diversity, unity; and here it comes not only to one God instead of a million, unifying and catching the pulse of the grand harmony of things, but Spirituality begins to work as a force in the percipient mind, — thus higher and higher. We cannot tarry longer on these points.

But in the third place, the law of Revelation is

such that God gives himself, reveals himself to the world just as fast as the world can bear Him. Why, even here, late as the time of Jesus Christ, He said: " I have many things to say unto you, but ye cannot bear them now." You cannot understand now, but by and by you shall understand them. And this higher preparation consists in your interior *subjective development;* in the opening of your eyes; in the unstopping of the ears of your soul; in the waking of your reason; in the quickening of your conscience; in the development and maturing of your whole inward being.

In the fourth place, God gives every revelation that He makes in such a way as to *compel study.* He gives himself in the hint form, in the figure form, in the symbolic, in the parabolic form; in such a way that you are obliged to seek, and to seek with all your heart—heart meaning the whole man—if you find. God did not propose to raise up a race of sloths or sluggards or moral sponges, making it a virtue that they have not dishonored God by doing anything themselves. That is not the way of his wisdom; but dig for the hidden treasure; toil night in and out, and day in and out, without ceasing. " My Father worketh hitherto," said the Master in the very law. And revelations are given not only so as to compel study and search, but they are not given in any infallible form, as if to save man from the possibility of making a mistake. He *can* mistake, and will mistake if he is not up to time in his duty. Thus the law of Revelation is such as to cultivate the sense of responsibility, cultivate the moral nature as well as the intellectual.

In the fifth place, it is a law of Revelation that the scale of its advance shall be, if you let me use the word—and the sooner we learn it the better—cosmical. I like to see an idea condensed into one word, instead of being spread over a hundred. It is the law of Revelation, then, that this scale of advance shall be *cosmical;* I mean that it shall be in fraternal sympathy with the great heart of all things, the great divine fellowship of all God's thinking and purposing in creation, in providence, in redemption. The matter of Revelation, my friends, this matter of religion, is not one you can take up between thumb and finger, a mere patch, sterile at that, detached from some corner of your existence. The scale of advance, higher and higher — higher and higher — must be the scale of the universe, breaking faith at no spot with aught in God's great scheme.

And in the last place it is a law of revelation that its benefits shall be *cumulative;* that is, hold all you get, and get all you can — not rest upon any single possession or conquest, but making all the base from which to push out still further aggressions — hold it as so much to which a great deal more is to be perpetually added. And thus we think of Revelation and its laws.

Now here we strike the great law of progress. Many a mind has caught that idea already. The law of progress! What is that? Nothing but the law of the nature of things. Note how this is asserted in *science*. Science tells us that the world was created progressively. Some men, in attempting to get hold of the cosmogony of the Hebrews, tell us that at first there was nothing but mist, nebulæ; and then out of that grew, progressively, order, stars, worlds, until there came to be the solid fact which we have now in the heavens. No matter what theory may prove true at last, we are not at the last yet; the grand primary truth will stand, that science asserts this great fact that God has manifested himself in creation progressively.

History asserts the same thing. It does it in the fact that history is a growth from a seed started, so to speak, from a germ, and carried on to the development and unfolding of its life more and more diversely, branching and rising towards maturity. This law of progress is asserted in all the *religions* of the world—the whole of them. I instanced the lowest, and then the next highest, and then the next, and so on to the end. Even the Old Testament from first to last shows this ascending scale, reveals this law of progress. God does not talk to the world, in the opening chapters of Genesis, as He talks in the time of Moses, as He talks in the time of the Kings, as He speaks in the old Prophets, and in the old Poets and Philosophers. An ascension—a grand growth of utterance appears; also an assumed developed capacity in the world to hear. And when you go out of the Old Testament into the New, and the New into the Old, the New stands as much higher than the Old as Monotheism stood higher than Polytheism — as a man stands higher in his work in life than the child with its playthings. It does not follow that the Old Testament enunciates the New, any more than the man enunciates the child, or the child the man. The question is, whether we see it; if we do, we can talk about it; if not, better talk about something else.

And now, right here is where we should be wise. Because there is a law of progress, the world of religious thought is greatly stirred. Old things are passing away that were once thought sacred to the heart, like the early drapery of children and their wooden horses — grand and divine so long as childhood lasted. But the world is nearer manhood than ever before; and in the ages to come it will be vastly nearer than it is now. What I am saying is, that the very stirring of thought, recasting of thought, not only in religion but in all things to-day, is born out of this everlasting law of progress, which is the law of God's manifestation of himself in the world. The great stress of the mind to-day touching religion is, to see how religion may be grounded in the nature of things; how faith may take the hand of reason and go down to this everlasting solitude, over which phenomena may drift forever and ever without disturbing it. So that this law of revelation, being the law of progress you perceive, teaches that *institutions* are good until they are outgrown; and after they are outgrown they are just as bad for the world as a child's clothing is for a man, or his playthings for the implements of mature industry. The same law of divine revelation tells us also that we have no occasion to fear *science;* that science is no disturber of real, everlasting religion. It tells us that science is a form, one of the chapters of the whole revelation of God.

This law tells us also, when we go back, when we make our pilgrimage rearward, we don't go to get *forms,* we don't go to the tribunal of phenomena for authority. We go back for essences. We go for that which is the same yesterday, to-day, and forever; for the root, the seed; the divine, not the human; for the eternal; the immutable, not the changeable. Then it is beautiful to go back. But the same law of revelation tells us, also, when we cast a glance ahead, it is not for the sake of cutting clear of the present or the past; it is for the sake of the better enunciation of all that was true and abiding in the past; for the sake of the more practical handling of all that we have on hand to-day. God is not a wild license in Himself, in his laws, in his methods. He is orderly. He is conservative as He is radical, and radical as He is conservative. Things hold together forever and ever. Things are vital forever and ever, for God is not a great automaton. Therefore He is radical; therefore He is conservative. Thus we find God always in the world. He never went out of the world. In all places, not only in the height and in the depth, but here on the lip, in the heart, He is, if we have the discernment to find Him.

There is a theory of the world called the mechanical theory, the purport of which is, that God made the world as a grand system of law and order and power, wound it up, and then left it to run itself. There is no life in it. It is a dead machine. It goes as well without God as with Him; and the theory was devised in order to get rid of the necessity of a God. Now, that is not the Christian idea. The Christian idea is, that God not only created the world, but that He is putting forth the selfsame exertion eternally which originated it. In Him the world not only began, but constantly lives, and moves, and has its being. God is creating now as well as at first, and will be; otherwise, this created finite perpetuity of things would relapse into non-existence. We see, also, that every age has its particular lesson given it to learn; and we see likewise, that each age can learn its own lesson. Every time, every period, every section in Providence, is like a recital in a school. The lesson to be got is mastered, and the end to be found out is God, so much of God as is manifested at the time. It can be done; and hence it is that God does not condemn one age for not conforming to another. The old Hebrews were not to be condemned because they were not Christians after the manner of Matthew, Mark, Luke, and John. And the New Testament men are not to be condemned because they do not conform to the standard of the Old Testament, or any other religion. Each age must be true to the lesson set for it and in it. God demands that, and has made it possible. Be true to your life-hour, O soul; and the greatest and the grandest can do no better. Time is one long revelation space, one long self-declarative scope of God, one grand manifestation of Him in work, in providence, in love; and the end is not yet. You cannot find a book in history or theology that limits time, creation, love, revelation, and the manifestation of God. There is no such book but a foolish one. It is impossible in the nature of things. The end is not yet.

In the light of such thoughts, we see plainly that if a man wishes to validate what he believes, if he wishes for a foundation to erect his faith on, he must not seek it in the human element of revelation. He must not seek it in the phenomenal element, but in the essential element. He must not seek it in the material of history, but he must seek it in that which makes history. So I am not disturbed, as I before hinted, when the critics come and tear this Book all to pieces. So far as my faith is concerned, it matters not whether the Book exists or not, as to the essence of things. The critic may find faults and flaws in history on the assumption that history is logic. He may find the same fault with the Bible, with the pictorial, figurative, childlike playthings of the Old Testament, that the mathematician found in Paradise Lost. He said he could not see, for his life, what it proved. It did not prove anything, because it was a poem ; not a syllogism, but an inspiration blossoming out with ideas, and with revelations too profoundly deep for the handling of logic and dialectic limitation. If you wish to validate your faith, don't go back to any form of words or facts that any man has brought into existence, that any body of men have voted. If you want to make a creed for the whole world, wait until the evidence is all in. You had better put that work off until you get into the light above. A creed is a verdict predicated upon all the evidence pertaining to the case, or else it is a false one. The God instinct, as well as the self-instinct, has always been in the world, and always will be; and you must provide for it if you are a philosopher, a thinker, a believer.

Look at Christianity then. Just here, let us ask ourselves what claim Christianity has, after all, over and above any other religion. If God is revealed in every chapter of providence, what is the pre-eminence here? What claim, let us ask, has the curriculum for the university, devised by the best scholars of the world, over the curriculum for the nursery, or the preparatory school, or the public schools in the various wards? The claim of fitness, evidently.

Just look at Christianity and mankind, and see how it fits as no other religion does. When a man looks into this mirror, he sees his face with its wrinkles, blotches and all, as no mirror ever flashed him back to himself. See the elements of universality in Christianity, which you find nowhere else. If God is developing one connected scheme, we should infer, from the mere necessities of reason, that a religion pertaining thereto must include the elements of universality. Christianity assumes to fill all places and all conditions and all fashions of human life and character. Then take the ethical principles of Christianity. We find them validated in the nature of things. They do not rest on phenomena. Histories that talked about them and revealed them may perish; yet the ideas and the great principles will stand, because they are rooted in the nature of things, and back finally in God.

The Christian religion gives us, in addition to a purer morality, a truer culture than any other religion. This is a grand thing. It assumes to handle men's nature, develop its undeveloped powers, mend its broken possibilities, and reconstruct the grand whole as no other religion assumes to do. And then, finally, it has in it the transcendental element. I mean it assumes to hold things by some power that transcends this life. Time, nature, all things seem holding over, linking man to immortality. That is its transcendental element. No other religion has this as the Christian religion has.

Now you will please take notice that, for any man to leave that which is better for that which is worse, proves him not a sensible man; shows him a bad thinker, not a true philosopher. He is not even a respectable scientist. You will notice again, to leave the better for the poorer, the higher for the lower, is to leave the living God and go back to the dead God. I mean to the mortuary records — to the footprints — back to those old forms and conditions out of which life has come. All true thinkers determine their thought in the last and best things. God in time and providence reserves to the last in form that which is first always in conception. In truth, the

Alpha and Omega are one in nature and design. While the Alpha becomes a husk, an autumn-leaf rotting and perishing, the Omega waxes strong, and towers and sings in triumph towards higher assertions and expressions.

There are several things that need to be emphasized just here, as coming from the train of thought we have pursued.

First, O soul, never throw away what you have, poor as it is, until you can get something better; and remember that the better is not to come from that which God has left behind, but from that which He has yet to give the world. Keep your faith awake, looking toward the East whence light arises.

Secondly, If you seek to do such work, never ground your faith on phenomena, but in the nature of things.

In the third place, keep your religion in high sympathy, as I said a little back, with the whole universe. Treat your religion as if it were a legitimate child of the Father's House, not a foundling by the way. Treat it as if it were a brother to every truth in the great family of truth; as if it were kin and kindred, having the very life-blood of the whole. Keep your religion warm in such sympathy, and you may depend upon it, it will grow — it will thrive.

Again, in the fourth place, be true to the law of *correlation*. What do I mean by the law of correlation? The law that tells you if there is such a thing as the eye, there is something for the eye to see; the law that tells you if there is such a thing as hunger,

there is such a thing as bread. Be true to this law,
or you are wrecked. Men get into trouble here.
They say, sometimes, all we need to know is inside
of us. All there is, is "consciousness." They might
as well say, All there is of the bird is his wings, no
need of air; all there is of the fish is his fins, no need
of the sea; all there is of man is his stomach, no
need of bread. Be true to the law of correlation.
What avails it for a man to say, I do not see light,
if he has a blind eye? What avails it for a man to
say, I am poor and have nothing, therefore there are
no riches in the world? Don't be so foolish as to
say, because your purse happens to be empty, there
is no such a thing as gold in existence. You are a
purse in yourself. You may be empty, indeed, but
you were made for something. Be true to the law of
correlation, and it will guide you through the storm—
through all revelations. It will hold you to God as
the anchor holds the ship tossed on the waves.

In the fifth place, rate every man for what he is
worth, and conclude that he is worth just so much
as he conquers in these grand lessons which God
sets him to learn. Just so far as he conquers these
by search, by reverence, by love, and by the use of
all the faculties and powers within him, just so far as
he comes to know God behind all revelations, and
takes Him into his *character*, has he manly worth;
and no further.

Now a great many may ask, what is the use of
preaching of this kind? What is the benefit of such
sermons, talking of philosophy, talking of science,

talking of ideas? One use is, it keeps the brain alive and saves us from the scandal that a man's brain withers and decays in religion as nowhere else. It keeps the brain alive; it keeps the man awake, at any rate. I venture to say every one who has followed closely this train of thought, has not nodded once; you have not drowsed, you have not even hung the head in fatigue. Familiarity with God as he is revealed, his thinking in creation, in providence, in our history, in our revelations, his great sympathy in the world, induces infinite wakefulness and stimulation in his creatures. It is good for that at least. Then these are the matters in hand to-day. I might bring before you every Sunday what was decided as essential to salvation in those old councils fifteen hundred years ago, which the Œcumenical Council at Rome has recently attempted to saddle the world with, and make essential to salvation for the next fifteen hundred years. I might bring these things out and make them the staple of my preaching. I don't know how it would be with you, but a great many would think it the true thing; a great many would not agree thereto.

There is a law of advance in religion, even in preaching. Dogmas and institutions are good until the world has outgrown them. The great effort of that Council was to anchor the nineteenth century back to the ninth; to send the world backward, not after God, but after man, to the devices which he happened to think of God. Now to handle matters in this more modern way is, I think, to meet a want of the times; and you will see it more plainly when

I give the next reason, viz: that if religion does not take the lead in interpreting God and interpreting man, something else will take the lead. If the pulpit and the pews eject the nature of man in relation to God from its subjects, and refuse their handling admission, then mark this: The platform and the press and the academic club will take charge of the matter and lead the thought of the world. If he who pretends to believe in God, and draw his faith from God, is not able to show a reason for that, and how all this life and the principles of the universe stand related to God, somebody else will show a life and a universe, and *another* reason, that will leave God out. And religion, as we now profess it, will just have to turn antiquary and go to the rear, or stand as a wallflower while the living play goes on. Such are reasons why the pulpit should do its own work.

The priests of old, you remember, asked Galileo why he made such disturbance in the world. Are not all things settled? Were they not settled in that council, and in that creed, and in such formularies? The idea that this whole grand scheme of worlds somehow or other is related to God, and is singing his name, shining out his glory; why, you are upsetting all the theology that has been settled for the last thousand years, said the priests of his day. Nobody else said it. What are you doing, said the theologist only a generation ago — certainly within two — what are you doing, O, geologist? You go down into the earth and make it after a new fashion, and then come up here and upset Genesis, arraying science against revelation. Anxiety was not aware that science is itself a book of revelation as well as other books. But what is the upshot of it all? Why, all Christendom has come to shake hands with Galileo; and all Christendom has come to shake hands with geologists; while there are other hands still to be shaken. God has not stopped. He has not left the world. He is not done telling what he thinks. He is not done building man, building providence in the world. He is at work, and ever at work.

Take heed, O Kings and ancient Bishops. Ask the people why they are making this turmoil? The people will answer: There is a law of progress which is the law of God, which is the law of history, which is the law of mind; and that is the law of motion and commotion. The old past is always muttering and complaining of the present, and much more of the future; while the grand truth is, God ever lives, the same yesterday, to-day, and forever, leaving the things that are done, and talking Himself out into the things that are before.

Yes, God empanels a new jury in every generation. He empanels a new jury in every case of thought, of truth, of faith, to be tried. It is not within the prerogative of the old verdicts to nullify or limit the jurisdiction of to-day. No: God is not done revealing Himself yet. Let us be true to the lesson on the blackboard for the recitation-hour. Let us give ourselves to the study-hour, asking most of all the meaning of the lesson in hand. That will root us, for the time, in God and in his Divine methods; and by and by, when He has something more to say which heart has not conceived, you and I shall blossom on the boughs of that higher expression. We shall sing there if we root in Him instead of rooting in man, in the temporal, in the human, and in the perishable. Books shall moulder away, and the moth shall eat the very Word that speaks the high Name. Nature shall crumble, time shall wane and come to an end; but God shall live, sing, and be God in higher manifestation after the sun has ceased his shining, and the heavens are rolled together as a scroll. Happy will he be whose thought, renewed, quickened, purified, reconstructed and developed, shall be able to look at God and see Him face to face, as now he sees Him only in part. But not less happy is he who can see God in the bright light hour, and understand Him in every lesson of his life set for him to learn.

I happened to take up a book, last evening, in a book-store, in whose opening preface I read this:

"The work of creation and redemption is a unit. The purpose of God in creating man ran through all history and all the works of nature, looking to man to be recreated and revitalized, that at last man himself might shine in the very image of God, and sing the hidden sweetness of his heart."

That was not the language, but that was the thought. And I felt cheered, that one of the leading and living Christian thinkers of the hour flanked the leading idea of my last fifteen years' work. I took it as a solace, not as a boast. And if we will put our sensitive fingers upon the life of public thought anywhere, we shall feel the pulse of this truth throbbing as a leading symptom. I pity men who run away from the living hour and opportunity at their door, and think that they are doing pious service by gnawing at the old bones of dead ideas and obsolete expressions.

Open your faith, then, broadly, Christian thinker and Christian believer. Open your prayers so broadly that they shall take in the fragrance and the quick inspiring life of the whole summer of God's visitation to your world. God is coming, ever has been coming, ever will be coming, more and more. The original Name hidden in Him, "I am He who shall be, the coming One," is ever true.

We have touched some of the laws of God's manifestation; we have hinted at the grand end; we have pointed at the great lesson of duty. Life and the universe are not atheistic. God lives in them, and is living through them unto you. True believer, your soul shall be the grandest revelation of God at last. It shall wear a crown of glory bright and resplendent, before which all the glory of God's manifestation in time shall be nothing but shadow.

Follow back the hints, then, wherever you can; gather them from the lips of the Master, from the writings of the Apostles, from old Prophets, from History, from Providence, through all Creation; gather up these hints and trace them back, back, back, until you come to their source. And then, having touched God by your own spirit, let that spirit touch and quicken yours. So shall you, glory-lit in the splendor beyond, be the last, final word that God shall speak for Himself.

IV.

THE ONENESS OF RELIGION AND THE RACE.

> *He hath made of one blood all nations of men for to dwell on the face of the earth, and hath determined the times before appointed, and the bounds of their habitation.*—Acts of the Apostles xvii. 26.

THIS is the text—but if we read the next verse, we shall see the purpose of it, namely: "that they should *seek the Lord*, if happily they might feel after Him, and find Him, though He be not far from every one of us."

Here is a grand and graphic statement of man in his relation to this mundane state of things. The object of it is distinctly hinted, and especially the high feasibility of the attainment of that object.

It seems that man is *one*, from God's point of view; one in nature, one in design. Man, wherever he is individually, is man universally, in the constitution, in the capacity, in the intent of his being.

But equally true is it that in his circumstances he is diverse; his habitation is appointed; his condition is specific and ordained in the very scheme of his being. Men differ on the ground of individuality, in their aptitude and specific fitnesses; differ as to their geographic relation, origin and capacity. They are born in different centuries; dwell under different climates; contend with and overcome diverse forces;

and work out specifically, and instrumentally, diverse ends.

But as man is one in his nature, and as religion is a birth of that nature on the human side of the question; — I once before said that, and a "single-eyed" man went and reported me as declaring that religion was of human origin entirely; — but the great truth will stand and bear repeating, nevertheless, that religion, on the human side of the problem, is a birth from man's nature, an inborn, innate necessity of his spiritual being, just as hunger is an innate necessity of his body; — since, I say, man is one, and religion an outbirth of his nature, why is not religion one?

We reply, religion *is* one. Notwithstanding, according to history and observation, it is so broken, diverse, and conflicting, it is *one* at the *root*. When we are radical, original, human and divine enough, we touch the oneness of this great truth in human nature. Let us handle it in various aspects.

Imagine — and there is no violence in the supposition — that some superhuman intelligence from another bright sphere should visit this earth, and stand in the presence of all the nations made of one people, and begin to question them. Think of him as first addressing them thus: "O ye nations, men of time, do ye all believe in man, in *humanity?*" "Yea," is the quick response, "we all so believe." But the question goes on, "Do you believe in *religion?*" And the murmur goes up like the breaking of many waters: "We all believe in religion." "Yes," continues the interrogator, "but have you all *sacred books*, have you all Bibles, have you all Scriptures?" "Indeed we have," answer the Hindoo, the Persian, the Hebrew, the Christian, and the rest. " You say that you have these," continues this inquirer; "but then I ask, have you all *revelations* from a higher world?" "Yea and Amen," is the quick answer, "we all claim to have revelations; that is the way our books come in the main." But closer than that the question is put: "Do all ye, who have your religions and your books, believe in the Divine *inspiration* of those books?" "We believe in nothing else; we all claim it, and it is set down in the books themselves; it is maintained by all the prophets of our faith." "Possibly," says the visitant; "but have you, all of you, *miracles?* do you all *believe* in miracles? have your books and your faith been tested by miracles?" "In every case," is the prompt reply. "You have but to read our sacred books to find it so; there is no historic religion in the earth that does not claim the validation of miracles." "Oh, indeed," continues the questioning; "but is it a common faith with you all, that virtue is better than vice? that your religions have a bearing upon the hope of some better condition of your humanity by and by?" "Even so," is the unanimous answer here.

But the great questioner advances: "I perceive you all agree in the main; are all of one mind, one faith, one family; brothers all; but are you at *peace* with each other?"

Here for the first he strikes a discord. "No, no, great visitor; we all quarrel; there is no agreement whatever between us; we deny each other; we are in antagonism; we excommunicate each other."

Such is the confession. The Mohammedan looks upon the Christian and calls him "infidel." The Christian looks upon the Jew, and pronounces him God's outcast wandering in the earth. The Jew denies the Christian faith, believing that to be idolatry, the last profanation in Jewish sensibility. The old Hindoo cannot tally with the Persian; and the Egyptian breaks faith with them all. And so they differ.

But leave everything else and come to the Bible alone; how there? We find at once that its devotees are broken into two great parties. One professes to believe the Old Testament simply; the other takes both the Old and the New, and they fight it out on that line.

If now we drop one-half of this contention, and come simply to the Christian side, we find that also broken into two. They all believe in the same Scriptures; in the same miracles; the same inspiration and revelation; but yet are divided; the Catholic denying the Protestant; the Protestant protesting through and through against the Catholic.

If, however, we lop off one-half of this antagonism, and take simply the Protestant side of it, where we should expect homogeneity, fraternal sympathy, if anywhere—what do we find? Infinite diversity; all broken up into denominations, sects, cliques, each striving to get the better of the other. One denies what the other asserts, and sometimes *because* the other asserts it. And thus it is with this last result.

By this time the angel visitant is confused and takes his leave, meditating upon the tangled problem of this religious conflict between the children born of one parentage.

But whence this conflict? I will tell you. It comes from putting the *accident* in place of the *essence;* it comes from treating the saw and hammer as though they were the temple; it comes from taking the sign for the thing signified; from putting the circumstance in place of the substance; man in place of God.

But is all this broken diversity useless, or worse than useless? By no means, if we rightly estimate it. It is providential. It is set in the order of things by Him who appointed the diversity of habitation and endeavor everywhere apparent. And the moment the world comes to *see* this fact, the compatibility of unity with diversity, one spirit with endless administrations, old rigidities begin to relax; asperities soften; persecutions and anathemas melt away; men break their exclusiveness, and thought becomes genial and fraternal. For each sees in every other a common origin and design; each sees, underlying the whole, the grand *universal principles* and purposes struggling for dominion. So inspired by the perception of these are the contestants now, that they are ashamed to remember their old bickerings, though when they knew nothing else, contention was their worship.

The moment the providential intent becomes manifest, there is the beginning of a new era in the mind.

Just look abroad upon the earth and see how religion has been necessitated to this very diversity. No such sacred book as this Bible could have been given to the whole world at once — to the men who have *other* sacred books; and theirs given to the race and age of the world that asked for the Bible, would have been an anachronism, a thing out of time. Revelation is progressive, and adaptation is one of its laws. The moment we distinguish between the circumstantial and passing away, and the substantial and abiding, old interpretations begin to fall off, giving place to broader and better ones; some things in the books themselves, that we have considered so sacred and so essential, are destined to pass away like autumn-leaves when the fruit is ripe. The provincialisms of religion come to an end in the growth of the world, and the mind and heart broaden out into great cosmic currents and orders of things. The original, fundamental, underlying ideas and purposes touching man in connection with religion, rise to self assertion, and are glad to get utterance in the faith and convictions of a broader intelligence. The essentials become more and more, and the non-essentials less and less. The diverse sects and denominations, churches and creeds, begin to open their closed doors for outlets and inlets, permitting them to swing both ways. Amplitude of faith and conviction knock down the old partition walls; there is an interchange of manhood and brotherhood among the children and nations bearing one blood and one purpose. The underground connections, the vital telegraphs, begin to exchange messages and to organize. As there is oneness in essence, so there comes to be more homogeneity in expression. And the world's fight grows less and less.

But another great question arises in the handling of these matters. Will the time ever come when all these external distinctions and diversities shall disappear never to be heard of again? No: that time will never come; it need never come. But this is what will take place: Men will cease to put the circumstance for the essence, the letter for the spirit; they will put things in the right places and call things by their right names. Things which can and should fraternize will wax stronger and stronger; while the elements of hostility will die out. The grand diversity will be increased even like the parts of a chorus, making the harmony richer; but the discords will drop out. Every man will be allowed to sing his own part, play his own instrument, and wear his own face, without being excommunicated for it. Each will know the other as his brother by the elements of brotherhood, not by clothes or creed or geographic position. Every man will be allowed to have his own interpretation, and for that reason will not think of denying that right to any other man. Possibly they may both be true. Fraternally they may stand and work on a broader foundation for their difference. The great, universal, primal principle of love to man will grow mightier; love to God will assert itself with more powerful sway; and love for truth because it is truth, will surpass all other passions. The universal will increase; the accidental decrease.

Now, what men want in this world just at this time, is to *know* each other; and not stand fenced off in isolated corners, peeping over their ramparts and shooting out their challenges and drawing return fires. They want to know each other; exchange salutations; look each other in the eye; look inside of each other. They must examine the old family records; inquire, whence is my neighbor? why walled off there? who is he? whither is he going? Then the mystic etching of the heraldic device will begin to blush up, revealing the old common ancestry. Then men will exclaim, "We are children of one Father, after all; we have no right thus to be Ishmaelitish towards each other; let us eat and drink and be friends together."

It would seem that our own nation at this particular time, has a great mission to perform in the way of God's providential usher to introduce strangers to each other. It is as though God, through us, were holding a grand reception, sending out the summons to the ends of the earth: "Come, all ye who are of a common origin, come bringing your faiths, your books, your traditions, your humanity. It was a wise forethought, which I always regarded as a *providential inspiration*, that the founders of our Government excluded all religious partiality from its Constitution; made no distinction, offered no favoritism, but gave one common protection to every faith under the sun. I hope the Government may never swerve from that policy. The Government was born at the bidding of those *fundamental principles*, a statement of which we just supposed the angelic visitor to evoke from mankind; it is founded on them, not on the circumstances of any book, or creed, or miracle, or anything of the sort. It is founded on *man* as he stands related *essentially* to his fellow-man and to his God. Let the Government stand firm right there. Never sign a petition, friends, that it may vary from that purpose.

True catholicity of thought is abroad in the world. The nerve of intelligence is receiving and sending telegrams every hour from this deep underlying network of principles and ideas, that make the race one. The brain leaps and the heart leaps — at first in delirium, indeed, and there will be commotion until they come to grand balanced serenity and power. The nations are awakened; the tide-wave of intellectual and spiritual earthquakes is rolling underneath, rocking the surface. No man can live hereafter, and be a narrow, stinted bigot in the world. The very remnants of the nobility of thought will hunt him, as an escaped spectre, back to his den. No brain can live walled up, when the time has come for the wall to be broken down. No heart can expand and throb with noble pulsations, that sticks to its flower-pot economy too long. Its roots want, and must have, the range of all the earth for truth and life and nurture. No stinted and bigoted sectarian has a mission after this, save as a kind of providential whetstone for the Damascus edge of God's truth and spirit. No nation can live a mere provincialism, walled up, set off by itself. Just look at the waking and breaking of the oldest nations on the earth. China is among us; Japan is coming; India is on the way; and out of Egypt will be called citizens and sons in due time.

No Church has any call or any mission on the earth in this hour of the world, that is fixed to some old creed, or dogma, or ecclesiasticism of some self-constituted censorship or conceited primacy. There is no infallibility from Pope to Puritan. The infallibility of God and truth you and I are to acknowledge; feel after, if haply we may find it; while to man's usurpation we only say, *Procul, O procul este profani!*

I often think there is more breadth, more world-breadth of thought outside of technical religion than inside; whereas religion *should* hold the broadest thinking in the universe, because its main element is infinite. What is the secret of the rejection of Christianity on the part of a great many finely-thinking, finely-mannered, finely-lived men and women in the world? Why do they stand aloof from religion? Why do they take opposition to it? For its own sake, think you? and because of those fundamental principles of it, which the angelic visitant evoked? Not at all. Men are religious by nature. These outsiders drop certain interpretations that religious insiders stick to; but religion itself they revere. Men of thought refuse allegiance to the mere accidents and self-constituted standards of hierarchies, sectarists, and dethroned gods, but not to the King of kings.

I have thought sometimes that it would not be the strangest thing that anticipation foresees, if God in his providence should raise up a Church in the future that shall organize Christianity on a broader basis, inclusive of all the grand fundamental principles of Providence, Revelation and Creation. And if that time ever does come, I doubt not some of the profoundest thinkers and believers that cannot get inside the Christian Church of to-day, will be among the priesthood and the elect of that new order of things. If that time ever comes, it will be because a broader welcoming of truth shall have sucked out the juices of the old schemes and policies, leaving them to wither like dry trees on the mountains, and building a new living kingdom in their place.

When men shot that magnificent enterprise across the continent, the Pacific railroad, and along its iron artery fresh blood began to throb and thrill from ocean to ocean, the old shanties by its side that the spademen occupied while they were building it, were deserted and abandoned. If now the old occupants had concluded to insist upon it that those huts were still, and always would be, the great centres of trade, they would have made the common mistake of many religionists. After that highway was cast up, and the continent veined by a new life-channel, nobody thought of entering the old shanties to live, save perhaps marauders and speculators on their own account, or some hostile Indian or other enemy of the road, opposed to progress, "squatting" there to put obstructions in the way. There is many a town in this country and in other countries, once flourishing and bidding fair to be the leading city of the region in which it rose, but simply because it did not fall into vital connections with the new channels of thrift, has shrunk not only to a third-rate position, but has been left to wither and dry up altogether. There can be no great city hereafter not situated upon a railroad, or upon a great river channel, or upon some ocean shore. There must be *cosmopolitan connections* kept up, or there can be no development of life.

Now, a great many religious denominations, a great many churches, are just like these old towns and shanties. On the whole, they are left. New channels of truth are opened, but they do not welcome them. Providential highways are cast up, but they are not careful or interested enough to form connections with them. The train goes on, and they meditate in isolation, decay and pass away.

Such is the order of things. It ever must be so. Highways are to be cast up, connecting ocean with ocean, continent with continent, nation with nation, in thought, in religion, and in civilization. The underground communications must be rife and glowing with vital messages; the invisible cords and nerves of universal principles must organize the world anew, and ever be making it new.

A great question arises just here: Will any religion ever become the universal religion? It is like the question: Will any language or any government ever become universal?

Doubtless some one will. But yet any such language will have its *dialects;* any such government will have its subordinate *municipalities;* and so any such religion, its distinctive administrations. Will the Christian religion become that universal religion, if there shall at last prevail such an one? That depends upon this principle, viz.: whether the Christian religion has breadth and capacity enough to take in every other truth of every other religion on earth. If its channel is broad and deep enough to receive and welcome every true affluent, if its genius be elastic and copious enough, it will lead the world; otherwise not. The universal principles are the ones I just referred to, when all the nations are assumed to answer back to the heavens — Yea and amen, we so believe. Lift them up, enthrone them; and if Christianity be great enough to include and wield them, she will become the universal religion at last.

Will the English language ever become universal? She is copious to-day, wonderfully so; and her bid stands higher this hour for universality than that of any other. But only as she has life and elasticity and catholicity enough to welcome and handle all the exigencies of human thought and sentiment and human necessity, will she lead.

Will our own government, or any government like it, prevail at last, and give a kind of oneness to civil administration in the earth? That depends upon the same principle. If it be broad enough, if it have capacity enough, if it have sufficient catholicity to welcome the whole social nature and necessities of mankind, then it will lead. If not, not. Such principles must determine, and they are worthy of the thought of every Christian statesman and scholar.

The problem of religion, then, is the problem of man himself. The great admonition is, enthrone the fundamentals at the beginning so that they shall become *universal* in the *end.* Then there shall steal upon this our life, peace and reconciliation; the alpha at first shall become the omega at last.

Then shall the swords be beaten into ploughshares, and the spears into pruning-hooks. The heart and brain of man shall come to the great rest-day, where work shall be without weariness, and praise without price. The scattered and dispersed tribes of faith and humanity shall be gathered together from their long estrangements, and be one in the earth — as they were one with God in the beginning.

In that coming day, which somehow or other we all believe in — the day of promise foreseen by prophets, sung by all the bards of time, the day of the world's jubilee; in that day, if the heralds thereof shall be seen to have been in the dawn-blush of our faith, in the day-star that hung in bright apocalyptic vision, then indeed are we, as a people, walking in dewy pathways, sacred and consecrated to Heaven. Well does it become us to exclaim, *What manner of men ought we to be?*

May the fidelity of our stewardship be equal to its greatness.

V.

IMITATION AND DEVELOPMENT.

> *He is not a Jew who is one outwardly; but he is a Jew who is one inwardly.* — Romans ii. 28, 29.

THE Jew, who is one outwardly, is a Jew of precedent and pattern; he is a copyist, a Jew of imitation. The Jew, who is one inwardly, is a Jew of the present and the future; he is a Jew of development, of progress. There is an external Judaism and an internal Judaism. My subject, then, this morning is, *Imitation and Development*.

We shall aid ourselves by attempting to clear distinctions. Imitation is external, while development is internal. The first is mechanical and artificial; the second, vital and original. One, you perceive, is strongly and emphatically personal; the other is entirely impersonal. Imitation is substitution for a thing; development is the essential thing itself. One is a shadow; the other a reality. One is exactly the man himself; the other the circumstances of the man. Thus for the distinction.

Now we see all things best in the light of pertinent illustration. Pass then, if you will, at any time, into a thrifty greenhouse in winter or summer time. There you see life in all stages, from the germ-seed to the floral crown and the finished fruit. There is *development.* Beginning internally, unfolding gradually, progressively, from stage to stage, all that was inward at first becomes externalized in manifestation at last. After that, step into a factory in France or elsewhere. There are piles of satin, piles of silk, piles of paint, piles of wire, various kinds of material, various kinds of skill — artistic, educated or uneducated; and the great business there is to make flowers out of that material, to make plants; to imitate the originals. It is an institution of *imitation.*

Pass into some of the great temples of the earth; they are covered on the surface with great, elaborate adornments; various colors and shades greet your vision. It is *fresco.* There is the form of the flower and its color; there is the cut and carved column; there is the double-grooved cornice, and the gracefully sprung arch; and nature herself seems not more articulate when she is speaking than this similitude — *imitation;* marvellous often. And after you have thus gazed, go out into one of God's forests. There is a seed seemingly rotting in the decay and mould of ages — a little germ. A beam of light bores its way through the branches and whispering leaves, and wakes up that primal germ. It develops; it unfolds; it organizes a knot here and a branch there, in the trunk and in the growth; and by and by the workman takes it when it is matured, and cuts it, and smooths it, and covers it with the mysteries of polish. Then you see the living *grain* of the wood. That is what nature has been about under the guidance of her own inspired genius. It is *development.* Follow, also, the architect as he begins taking the plan, which is nothing but paper and color, and see how he generates the cornice and the capital; and how he creates the arch and the column and the artistic whole in your presence, of that pile of beauty; and you will follow the *development* of the primal architectural conception. Here you have, indeed, *development*, as at the first, *imitation*.

Sometimes you go to the theatre or opera, or you attend in your houses dramatic exhibitions. You call them plays, imitations of whatever the original matter in hand may be. If it be the good Samaritan, everything is done that means that marvellous picture. This is *imitation*. And after you have witnessed it, go into the *Orphans' Home*, or out among the wounded and dying soldiers — there is the original drama. *That*, in its terrible unfolding, in its blood and tears and fire of passion and agony, is *development*. What we mean by development is the *life-drama* in all the acts and scenes.

Did you ever see a regiment or whole army on dress-parade? The equipments were all polished and glittering; everything was in taste and in order; all the motions exact. The dress parade is imitation; a make-believe of the army in actual duty; a sham fight, it may be, for the time parodying a real fight. But if you want *development*, if you want life in its struggles, in its self-manifestation and self-execution, go out upon the battle-field; go, if you possibly can, back to old *Waterloo*, back to *Marathon;* go to *Sadowa*, to *Appomattox*, to the *Wilderness*. There things are real; no imitation, but facts.

Children love to imitate; they delight in play, and you love to see them. They get their locomotives and their train connected, and they *play* railroad; they play school-keeping; they play legislative assemblies; they play life. That is *imitation*. But real life, the grand evolving problems of civilization from age to age, stage to stage — there you have *development*, because there you have life in its unfolding and progressive economy.

So that anything conventional, anything merely external, may be termed *imitation;* while life itself, in all its fortunes and phases and facts, is a life of *development*, of originality, of actuality. One is make-believe, the other is sober fact; one is man as he is, the other is man as to circumstances.

Now, I do not say that imitation is in every possible sense illegitimate. It has its sphere, as in childhood, in decorative and symbolic art. We do not question this. But if you would see imitation in its illegitimacy, which more especially concerns our topic at this time, then notice it in its applications. For instance, *Art*. Men of money sometimes buy pictures when they get nothing but copies. We are not all artists, and we cannot judge; so we must depend upon testimony. But how often we see described as the inspired production of some great master, some mere imitation, and poor at that. It is no work of genius. Art is development; art is evolution; art means the vital conception of beauty or truth, the progress of its unfolding in the mind of genius, until at last it stands all aglow in vision or tone, the realized form of perfectness in sense. It is never imitative. Art is always original. *Artifice* is not always original; usually borrowed.

Apply the distinction to *Literature*, and you see the same thing. What is the difference between the scholar and the student? A scholar is an imitator, while a student is an evolver. A student is one whose mind is in process continually of vital *development* from central personal germs of power. A scholar may know everything in the world, and be nothing in himself. A student may know scarcely anything, and be next to Omnipotence. One is the birth and maturity of power; the other, the machinery or instrumentality and the tools thereof.

So in *Morals*. A man may be pointed out to you who never tripped — the law was not sharp enough to catch him. He was rounded on every corner; so polished and smooth that the very rain of heaven would fall off from him externally like oil. Internally it may be different. Externally the platter is clean, nice and fine:— Imitation. Another man may be scarred all over, from the crown of his head to the sole of his foot, by conflicts of passion with himself; from the fights with evil outside; quick, strong, impulsive, explosive. He may be covered all over with the stone-marks made by those hard, sharp missiles which conventional morality threw at him, and the uncharitable judgments of men; while inside, where God's judgments frame their verdicts, the very fights he carried on with himself for the sake of the sublimest conquest, may have started germs of character and wrung out cries from his soul for help from God, that make him in the end a Paul, or a Peter, or a Luther. When the outward scars shall all be healed over by spiritual granulation from within, he shall be fair and pure as the angels. While a mere frescoed moralist, one who imitates right from the mere constraints of an outward conventionalism, may be inwardly festering with the virus of all uncleanness.

Apply the same thing to *manners* and you come to the same result. Who is a well-mannered man or woman? Somebody who has read Chesterfield? or somebody who understands court etiquette, or who has snobbed it around among the parrots and parvenus of social conventionalism? Why, the figures in the showman's windows can do it with fewer mistakes. Good .manners, high breeding, true quality of soul, gentle life — it is a culture, a growth. It comes not of imitation; it is a birth of graces and beauty and worth from within. It comes naturally, as blossoms come, answering to no prescribed pattern. A well-bred, well-reared soul is a copy of nothing. The gentle, living, genial, beneficent-hearted man or woman, pure as sunshine, is God-made, trained and developed in that school of higher tuition from which all humanity must draw its finest finish and expression.

Consider *heroism*. Did you ever see a mock hero, crying, "Don't be a coward!" Bravery at that rate is as easy as it is cheap. Who is the true hero? A man with firm and mute lip, with fixed eyes, with blanched face it may be, who can go down into the breeding charnel-house of disease, and from it project a sanative campaign that shall turn back the advancing waves of the destroyer, while he understands very well that it is at the cost of his own life. Who is the hero? He who, if necessary, cannot only walk up to the cannon's mouth when the battle is raging, but in some peaceful hour, for the sake of some grand victory out of which the jubilees of all time shall be made, can put the cup to his lip that shall make him missing forever. Who is the hero saint? Not he who brags of his virtue, and his excellence, and his prayers, and his sanctity, and sometimes his orthodoxy—but we will leave that out. The saintly hero is he who, in the face of scribes and pharisees, dares to tell the truth because it is the truth; who dares to do right because it is right; who can afford to be just at a cost, and make a record that shall paint no shame in his face at last; he has saintly courage who can do all this without fear, favor, or hope of reward. Such as this don't come to a man all at once. He can chalk it on the blackboard; he can dramatize it in symbols, stage effect, or altar practice; but that won't do. It must be an experience developed from within, of power and self-regency under the law of God, the only acknowledged higher law.

Charity. What is charity? Great pockets full of money? That indeed is excellent; still, what is charity? A mighty institution, a tract, a Bible, a missionary society, scattering beneficence as autumn-leaves fly? A kind of sentimental philanthropy, dispensing patronage as easily as it is acquired; whose best name is, after all, indifference? Nay, *this* is charity — the widow's mite, the great broad heart. The hoard of Crœsus *may* be charity. If it has a beautiful spirit, a spirit broad enough to take in all the margin of the great life-play, all the conflicts, all the joys, all the reciprocities of light and shade, singing and sighing, then wealth and power and glory may be charity. But this greatest of graces is an emancipated soul; a soul touched by the love of God; a high, mighty, suffering love of heaven; touched in its germ-centre, unfolded, unfolding, into personal experience; growing, developing, until it becomes a mighty fact, as God was a fact manifest in the world. Charity is help, sympathy, spontaneous, the result of a cultivated and disciplined character; never done by proxy, never reached by copying, never possible by transcript or imitation. It must be *born from within*. You cannot tell who is charitable or who is not, by appearances. The most charitable man that ever lived never told of it. The grandest exhibition of charity that has been on this earth — nobody knew much of it but the angels. Once in a while you see a case like Mr. Peabody, or Mr. Stewart — I speak of them as honorable men of course — who seem impressively charitable. And yet *real* c' arity is that which is home-born — born and reared in the way I am speaking of, whether it be known or unknown to the world.

Men have a passion for *eloquence*. What is eloquence? If men love anything in the world, it is to hang spellbound upon living, palpitating words and brain-throbs from some fount of genius and power. Who is the eloquent man, Demosthenes, Cicero, Burke, or Pitt? Who of our own land, Webster, Everett, Patrick Henry, or Henry Clay? Thoughts and words that speak and burn, and burn to speak, are born; they are a growth of utterance; they are an *evolution* of life and power. They ask no leave to be; they pattern after nothing; they are self-spoken. Mankind will live and be glad to hear and answer such.

Apply the same thing to *religion*. That was the application in the text. Who are the *saints* in the world? Are they those men and women who seem to suspect that it would never be suspected of them — I mean sainthood — but for the great and liberal advertisements which they often make, or attempt to make, of their goodness? Who are the saints? the men in dress parade, in fresco, in stage action, whether in church or out of church? experts at religious machinery — are those the saints? Was it St. Simon so called, who stood on the pillar till his very nails grew to be like bird's claws — was he the typical saint? Or shall it not be rather some poor unknown toiler and sufferer, who works the very nails off until his fingers bleed, for man, for truth, and for love's sake? Who are the saints, we again ask? the dogmatists who fill the world with noise and clamor and strife and blood, about mere names and words, about something which they think they must *imitate* from father or grandfather, from saint or apostle, or somebody else? Is he the saint, or the soul with Christly spirit, that don't know the meaning even of the battle-words with which he hews out mischief in the world? Who is the saint, we still inquire? Is it that closeted one at whose lips an invisible ear bends to catch the breathing, and to wing it away and tell of it up high? or is it he whose prayers, it may be, are so elaborate and ostentatious as to be troublesome to his neighbor? Is the true saint of the world the zealot of the past, who patterns and copies the t-crossings and the i-dottings, word for word and letter for letter? or the man and woman who know nothing about the letter, and care nothing about it; hungry only for the spirit, and for greater things to come? Are the saints they of the paint and toilet one day in the week? or they without any paint or any toilet whatever? but who fear God and do righteousness from Sunday to Sunday, and from Monday to Monday, living and dying.

Who are they that *pray!* Such as carry their prayers in their pockets, or in their hearts? Men who retail them off as the work of a machine, or who hide them for the most part, not only in the closet, but in the deep-glowing fires of the heart? Men consumed with the passion of desire — men divinely frenzied for emancipation from darkness, for liberation and freedom from the thralls and restraints of time and sin, that they may be in the liberty-chime of the Divine thinking? Such soul-agony does not perish; it is not cheap; it is not born all at once; it comes as summer comes out of winter; it comes as life comes out of death; *developed* from the sources of man's nature when touched by the life of the higher nature.

Who really *believes?* He who knows more creeds than you can count? he who makes more noise and trouble in the world about his orthodoxy than ever the Master did? and yet would be first to come under the impeachment of the chapter we read this morning? or he who knows nothing about such things, and cares nothing about them; but is in a state of suffering sensibility lest his spirit lose its purity, or his heart be soiled or compromised by evil? Who *really* believes? He who takes the *life* of Christ into his *soul?* or he who only takes the history of Christ, and how men have thought about Christ in other days? Is the true believer the one who is the subject of high and divine inspirations, so deep and profound that he cannot utter them and talk about them? or he who is so loaded and clogged with the mere theories and opinions of men on the subject, that he has no scope for anything else?

Who is really the *Christian?* Is it the punctilious, exact imitator of what is done and canonized and endorsed by other imperfect men? or he who goes forth with life and strives, as a conscientious man, to do everything he does, and think everything that he thinks, as an upright, true, honorable son of an all-perfect Father, hoping never to be ashamed of his record in the great end? The real Christian! It is easy to symbolize virtue, to symbolize our graces, to say if we dress in white it means so and so; if we dress in black it means so and so; if we do this, it means one thing; if we do that, it means another; if we read the drama and play the play, we acknowledge such graces and such virtues. It is easily done — very easily done. But to develop from the man himself this grand drama of purity and grace; of beauty, and truth, and glory; bringing it right out of him as roses are brought from winter and ice — that is not so easy. There is a mighty difference; one is *development* and *growth;* the other is *imitation, copy, simulation.*

Having, then, touched these distinctions and illustrations and applications, you have not failed, even of yourselves, to notice that we are in the midst of great *fundamental matters;* that we have touched vital, essential ideas and principles. In the first place, one is never *obliged* to be a copyist; he is never obliged to be an *imitator;* he is a free man, if he will use his freedom. Every man has an internal seed, a capacity of nature, a power, a competence, that *may be developed* into a true man — I don't say without God; but he has that subjective element in his nature which can save him from a mere parody, a mere imitation.

Then, when a man comes to a life of truth and self-development, he touches the *heart and harmony of universal things;* all that lives; the grand universal life of nature; perfectness in God. Every man who comes into this true personal life is in affiliation therewith. True *progress* lies here. How many are there ever learning, and never able to come to acknowledge the truth! This is the reason. They work externally; they work unvitally, in machinery, in signs, patterns, symbols, impersonalities. Truth must be born through their experience; they must have developed minds. Grand evolutions of God's thinking must come forth of them constantly. Then they will be ever learning, ever knowing more and more.

And here, in this process of true personal development, we come to organize the *life that is now, into the life that is to come.* A life of imitation will leave its copywork behind; the copyist will go naked into another world, poor, blind, naked in himself, being nothing. What we plead for strikes the vital cords, strikes the great arterial circulations that knit the two lives into one; and everything we do here rightly and divinely, shall last — we shall find it at the last day.

A man who lives in his religion as a mere copyist, a mere echo of other thoughts, and other opinions, and other characteristics, will surely come to those *exigencies* in life, where he will be found *wanting.* At his own tribunal he will lack balance, poise and self-control. He may have thought he was a saint; that he had deep trust in God; that he knew where his stay and staff were; but he will come to some great hour in which he will feel that he has been nothing but an imitation. Whereas a man who is truly developed, unfolded in his nature, coming into these stressful hours, will find that the cords are all taut; that the spars are all firm; that he has a stay and a balance in the storm. The deck may rock underneath him, but he is trimmed. The laws of the storm are for him. He has grown personally, experimentally. He has his allies in the great universal law of the perfectness of things.

Such a man is *somebody*, instead of a sign of somebody. Having taken God up unto him, he is more and more a true man. He is like a tree growing by the river-side; his nurture comes from the sources of universal truth and life. History no longer holds him her vassal; history is not his prison; it is not his authority; never his tyrant, she stands as his admonition; his warning; his tutor; but his master never. *One* is his master, even He whom all history owns. *Hope* is no longer an echo of the past, but a bright glimmer from out of the future. *Faith* is a deep, well-settled trust in the *order of things:* an order that is unbroken as the wisdom of God. Trust is a confidence in God that he will never play false. *Aspiration* becomes a prophecy now as well as a yearning in man's nature; and salvation, nothing but a sublime evolution of man out of the still primal germ with which God seeded his nature, now *fructified* by a Divine nature. I am speaking, you perceive, of manhood; of perfected man; developed, disciplined, inspired, regenerated, broad, living; of faith as a fact, or religion as a personal reality. *Heaven will be finished selfhood;* that finish that was ever heralded in the dream slumbers of creation and re-creation.

So that, following religion through the economy

of a vital evolution instead of dead imitation, we have a *beginning* which is the planting of God in your nature,— regeneration is a good word for it, if you take the spiritual meaning of the word. If you hold to the *process* of this planting in its development, which is the summer growth of God in your soul, then you come to the *end*, which is the ripening of God to the fruits of character unto immortality.

Thus we have set forth these distinctions; these illustrations; these applications; and these general co-ordinate principles.

Now for the *admonition*. Be *yourselves;* first, be yourself; next, be yourself; and last, be yourself; God only being greater, as He is your helper and your counsel.

Develop your *nature;* don't leave that to decay, die and rot, while you are busy, making great ado about the working of things on the other side; develop your *manhood* and *womanhood;* stir up your soul to life and fire down at the very germ, and quicken that. God is right here to help you. Unfold the God-given capacities within. You have such capacities. They are in God's image. Unfold them; make them larger, broader and broader; don't be satisfied because you think you are converted, and "saved." You are saved only so far as you are unfolded. A man would be foolish to think that because the tree has *sprouted* in the acorn, such is the end of the matter. Most likely the germ will die; it must die if it be not permitted to go on and fulfil the scale of its economy. So unfold this capacity of mind, of heart, of reason, of memory, of hope, of aspiration ; and as these capacities unfold, fill them with the *contents of God himself.* Let Him be poured into these empty cups of your nature. When the capacities for these flowers before us were opened, God came down and filled them; therefore they are not sham ; God is in that flower as in your nature ; as in the developed and broken heart ; divinity there for beautiful ends. I use the illustration for the sake of saying that this expansion, and developed capacity of your human nature, must be filled from the contents of the *Divine nature.* That makes you a reality, your true self, and not a mere copy or sign of something.

Then your life shall not wither however severe the drought ; and your root shall not perish however chill the winter. Then life itself will be a sublime eloquence, your very presence in the world being as the tongue of God, speaking high and beautiful things ; and death, when he shall come, will be only a kind of cæsural pause, where the last mortal paragraph ends and the immortal begins in this sublime utterance, which is yourself proclaiming the glory of God. Be yourself, then, and not another. Be entirely real, and true, and positive ; be no makebelieve, but a mighty faith and fact in your own personal right and estate ; and then you yourself shall be a new Word of God, vitally and divinely spoken.

Modern Jews of Jerusalem have, at the west side of the Temple, what they call a "*wailing place,*" where they go every Friday afternoon about three o'clock, and bewail the death of their nation ; the departure of its glory; the silence of its temples! O how much better would it be for that degraded people to turn away from the past toward the future, and let their cry be to God for the grandeur and glory of temples that are coming, by virtue of which the glory that was shall be nothing. The Christ and glory that they and we want, are ahead; something to be expected; and not what we hold in our memory. The Christ, the Gospel, the glory that we all want, is the coming *finished self*, unfolded from the primal germ of such infolded possibility as God wrapped up in the beginning of our existence. Men love to think of Heaven as a garden, a paradise — beautiful figure indeed. That garden is to be just where it now is, in your own nature; your own nature divinely developed and perfected. Why, then, go about picking up leaves from other gardens; from other men's experience; from past ages, when your own is full of divine buds and germs, if you only let them up into life and sunshine waiting to greet them and make them a garden immortal in the hereafter?

Development, then, means *inspiration* as well as *aspiration;* it means *taking in divineness*, breathing in air and summer as well as unfolding your native capacities. This is what we are pleading for. Be true, therefore, to this economy of the divine husbandry; be true to the vocation of your nature. Then, when the frescoes and the signs and the imitations are all done, and there is no Jew outwardly, you shall be beautiful; you shall be abiding in this state as God himself.

VI.

CHARITY.

And now abideth faith, hope, charity — these three; but the greatest of these is charity.
1 Corinthians xiii. 13.

IN the exquisitely beautiful and tender delineations of this thirteenth chapter, we have the masterpiece of Paul. For depth of insight, for profoundness of philosophy, for comprehensiveness of scope and intent, for gentleness of feeling, for vital pervasiveness of spiritual power, and fulness of statement as to the sum and substance of Christ and His religion, this chapter is not only unsurpassed by anything that Paul wrote, but unequalled by anything found among the writers of the Old Testament, or elsewhere in the New.

Here the heart of Christianity is purposely unveiled; the portrait of what the religion of Christ can make in human character, is presented intentionally; the divinity of the Christian religion, as it manifests itself in the working of the human soul, is the point of the painter's pencil. God's power in transforming and saving man, may be here seen in living, concrete fact.

In the previous chapter, the spiritual gifts and personal endowments best suited to promote the welfare of religion and the Church are pointed out.

They are mentioned as tongues, knowledge, the gift of healing, the power to govern, the power to work miracles, the gift of prophecy, the power of faith, skill in interpretation, and, at last, apostleship itself. We have it in such words as these: "To one is given the word of wisdom; to another knowledge; to another faith; to another healing; to another miracles; to another prophecy; to another tongues; to another interpretation of tongues; all by the same spirit." The chapter closes, after enumerating the gifts of healing, the gifts of interpretation, the gifts of miracles, and of faith, with the admonition, "Covet the best gifts;" and then, at the end of that, is added, "I show unto you a *more excellent* way." That way is detailed in the chapter following.

"What!" we are ready to exclaim from our education, from our associations from the very cradle up to manly and womanly life — "what! is it possible that there can be anything more excellent than *faith*, than hope, than miracles, than prophesying, and all the other spiritual gifts, not omitting apostleship itself?" Yes, there is something more excellent than any, or all. It is CHARITY. Its superior excellence is indicated after this fashion: "Though I speak with the tongues of men and of angels, and have not charity, I am as sounding brass or a tinkling cymbal. Though I have the gift of prophecy and understand all mysteries, all knowledge, and though I have all faith, so that I could remove mountains, and have not charity, I am *nothing*. And though I distribute all my goods to feed the poor, and though

I give my body to be burned, and have not charity, it profiteth me *nothing.*" All nothing! nothing! sounding brass and tinkling cymbals, all. Why? For "charity never faileth; whether there be prophecies, they shall fail; tongues, they shall cease; knowledge, it shall vanish away. For we know in part, and we prophesy in part. But when that which is perfect is come, then that which is in part shall be done away."

Here is something surpassing all other graces and gifts, in that it *never fails.* Here is something which, in the fading presence of all other brilliance and power, is perennial in its thrift and growth. Here is a truth and grace which, while earthy surface and mere lip accomplishments are fading, ebbing into the last hue and cadence, shall be waxing stronger and stronger, from childhood to manhood, from manhood to angelhood, until at last it shall shine as the face of God in the conscious fullness of completeness.

Last Sunday we tried to answer the question: What is it to be a Christian? and did not dare go far from the authority of Christ. Therefore we said: " He is a Christian, or she is, who *lives the life that Christ lived."* That doctrine is rejected, we know, to some extent; but when we must go among conflicting opinions, and take the risk of making our stand where matters are disputed, I think it is always best to hang upon the lips that spake as never man spake, and so trust the issue. Therefore I answered the question as I did. Here is the same question an-

swered in another form. Christ told men how to
live. Paul held up a specimen of what man is who
does live as Christ directed. We do not study this
matter, this actual, living part of religion, as we
should. We find ourselves hiding away in theory,
covering ourselves up in doctrine, or what we call
our beliefs or faiths, so far from real life often that
if our beliefs were contagious our lives would be
scarcely in danger.

And I seem to see a reason for this. I don't
blame myself altogether; I don't blame men generally for being in this position. Who of us does not
reflect the training, the manners, the habits of thought
we inherited in our first lessons? These matters
come upon us unconsciously; therefore, the fact that
we rule out of our religion so much practical life and
godliness, does not perplex me, for I seem to see a
reason for it, and in part an apology.

Notice that the religion and faith which we call
Protestant has, from the first, left this whole matter
of charity quite too much out of its doctrines. We
remember that the primal enunciation of the Reformation was " salvation by *faith alone.*" That grand
movement was constructed on military principles.
Opposition to what was assumed to be wrong in the
past, was its central force and purpose. The movement contemplated arrest of error more than development of truth. It was a protest, as the name implies. There come periods in the world when just
this sort of work is necessary.

One error the Protestant Reformation set itself to

correct, was that of *supererogatory* service. The reform under Luther could not endorse the idea that a man can work an extra credit mark, so that by virtue of that extra righteousness in service he may sometimes offset an indulgence. So the whole force of the movement set itself against that idea, and said: " No, not by extra service, but by faith alone does man win Divine favor." Then, again, the Protestant movement set itself to fight against what is called the abuse of charity. Almsgiving had become a mighty institution; and we Protestants are free to say, or ought to be, that in the dispensations of charity in the forms of almsgiving, looking after the poor and needy, succoring and uplifting the downfallen, the Catholic Church for centuries did a work that should put every Protestant face to the blush. But then we know that all men are alike, especially as seen in the fact that no man or institution can bear perpetual prosperity without running into dangerous degeneracy. Almsgiving became a means of wealth and power; or, to put it in better phrase, a grand system of *collection* for investment. Against that the new movement protested. Faith was the principle run up on every Protestant flag; nothing but faith, faith untarnished by works. And then Protestantism said there was a great deal of superstition lingering in the Church. It had risen to colossal dimensions; it had put its mighty grasp upon the vitals of Christ. That is what Protestantism professed to set itself to correct; superstition coming from Paganism; lingering shadows of it coming down from an elder dispensation.

Now, it is never any use to unhorse a wrong rider, and then, in leaping to the saddle, leap over to the other side; for you are off as much as your antagonist. Protestantism did it. This very day she is quite as deficient in charity and humanity as the Catholic ages were in spirituality and divinity. Salvation by *faith alone* rang out the thesis of the great Reformer; and the reverberations and echoes thereof fill the mountains and valleys of the nineteenth century. Salvation by faith alone — and this is just as much an error and superstition with Protestants, as was salvation by works alone with Catholics. Paul, of all apostles and teachers, is cited as authority for this faith-scheme. Paul was, indeed, in a very important sense, the Protestant of his day. His first movement and grand work was a protest against the errors of a former dispensation; and yet, if you will notice, when Paul comes to speak for himself on this very point of faith, what does he say? This, precisely: "There is something as much greater than faith in the matter of religion, as faith is greater than sight." There is something as much more important than faith, as truth and reality in religion are superior to "sounding brass and tinkling cymbals." When Paul comes to speak for himself, his grand word is: "Though you have faith that may remove mountains; nay, though you give your body to be burned," it is all talk, it is all "*nothing.*" NOTHING is the word he uses. Unless this foremost and fundamental grace impassion your soul, martyrdom and faith are not saviors at all.

Paul, by the interpretations of men, has evidently been perverted. Most unmistakably has he been misinterpreted; but that is not singular. We know, for example, how Paul has been set against James, and James against Paul; and how much sweat of rhetoric and lumber of logic have been spent as if they needed reconciling. It is easy to set up men of straw and then shoot them down. What is effected when you have reconciled James and Paul? Nothing; they were never at variance in their theology. Just so Paul has been set against himself. The polemics did it; and after they had professed to solve the difficulty which they had created, they only left the matter just where they found it. When this great faith-apostle is permitted to stand before the commentators and speak *for himself*, as he spoke before Agrippa in that personal vindication, what does he say? This, indeed: Faith is great and mighty, and enters as a force into salvation; hope is great and mighty, and enters as a force into salvation. "By faith ye are saved;" "by hope ye are saved;" and yet there is a greater than faith, or hope, or death itself, and that greater is — CHARITY. *They* are put in the background by him when he speaks for himself, while *this* comes to the front; and who shall say Paul is not more competent to speak for himself than we are to speak for him?

Protestantism, then, the reformation movement of three centuries ago, seeing what was to be done, seized the reins of infallibility from the hands of the Pope, and mounted the chariot of infallibility itself.

Then the grand old fighters, the stalwart theological leaders and polemics of that day, putting their own interpretation upon Paul instead of taking Paul's interpretation, lifted their flag and started their campaign. The whole movement was constructed on the polemic system, opposing and protesting against something assumed to be wrong. Instead of bowing to Paul as primary authority on the matter upon which he speaks, Paul was compelled to bow to the reformers; so that we in our day have come to read, as they did, this greatest of Apostles through the spectacles of other parties, instead of reading and judging of those parties through the eyes of Paul himself. And this is about the whole story of salvation by *faith alone*. No wonder that St. James said, "Faith alone is like a body without a soul, dead;" and dared to boast a little, constructively, in saying, " Show me thy faith without works, and I will show you my faith by my works." He did not discard faith, but he demanded that it should be living and productive. No wonder that Paul himself said afterwards, when handling religion in its practical, living form, " Work out your own salvation with fear and trembling; this God-power which is love-power working in you to will and to do." That is the motive, the inspiration, the why and the wherefore of the whole.

In that, Paul but repeats Jesus Christ himself. Christ told men how to live; Paul tells them what they will do, how they will appear, the fruits they will yield, if they do live as Christ directed. And here the two, Paul and Christ, come to oneness. The man of Tarsus and the man of Nazareth are one in spirit, in purpose, in result.

Jesus Christ said, when on earth, "A *new* commandment I give unto you, that ye love one another;" and on another occasion, putting it in a different form, He summed up all the law and the Prophets, the whole duty of man, in this one exercise of love or charity — toward God primarily, toward others as ourselves. The meaning of this word charity is simply LOVE. That is God's name in the Bible, and that is His nature there declared. "God is love," says the Book. This is the mission of Jesus Christ to our world. This is His Gospel of salvation. God Himself, who is love, so exercised His Godhood, that He sent this power of salvation in Christ into the world; and because He first loved us, the argument runs, we love Him; Divine love propagating itself in human love. Charity, according to this, is the very seed and root of all the graces and all final harmonious thinking. The charity of Paul is the love-power of God; the love-power of God is the incarnation of Christ; and Christly men are the fruitage and the trophies of this power.

Here then stand the mighty three, Faith, *Hope*, CHARITY; Faith grasping all coming possibilities; Hope throttling the old giant Despair; and Charity breeding in human nature the Divine nature. Hope is mighty; her lamp shall never be extinguished. Faith is great and grand; she shall live forever. These three are one in harmony and purpose, and the three shall reign for evermore. But the kingly glory of this trinity, you will observe, is not Faith; it is not Hope; it is CHARITY. This wears the crown. So speaks Paul, speaking for himself.

Follow, therefore, after charity. This is the more excellent way; this the kingly and queenly gift to be coveted; without this all other gifts are vain talk and specious disguise. Here is the theology of Christ, Paul and God, according to the New Testament; and here their religion. "Tongues shall cease;" "Knowledge shall vanish away;" the musical syllables of time shall ebb to silence; the crumbling foot-rest of the hour shall trickle from Faith; but there is something that is abiding, something that is lasting, something that is unfading. Men may have faith that shall "remove mountains," which is intended to be the mightiest and most exhaustive statement or conception of faith. Men may add thereto their own bodies to be burned; and after they have done it — what? Martyrdom itself, together with this mightiest faith, is *nothing*. Men may know all mysteries; they may believe in and work all miracles; they may turn true or false prophets, and speak like angels; yet without this God-name and God-nature in their religion, they are *nothing*.

This is the undeniable testimony of him whom men have vaunted as authority for salvation by faith *alone;* a testimony as explicit as it is conclusive, and which makes Faith, when compared with the greatness of CHARITY, fade and vanish into *nothing!*

Are the old superstitions all dead? Is Paul an infidel? Is the religion of Jesus a worthless rag?

VII.

CHARACTERISTICS OF MODERN THOUGHT.

> *The eye cannot say unto the hand, I have no need of thee; nor again the head to the feet, I have no need of you.* — 1 Corinthians xii. 21.

THE body is a system of related parts, organs, and functions. The eye is helped by the hand, and the head by the feet. Stomach, lungs and heart work together; so do bones, nerves and muscles. The whole is a beauteous unity made up from great diversity; strong and balanced on the principle of interdependence and supplemental adaptation.

The same is true of mind as of body. Memory, judgment, love, sorrow, reason, will, worship, work together in unity, each helping to complete the other.

So, also, in the whole realm of truth. Ideas are related, supplementary, interdependently. Goodness goes with wisdom, and beauty with both. Science, faith, art, virtue, beneficence, are a brotherhood. Each has need of the other and of the whole.

A recent vigorous Christian writer of Britain penned this incisive thought: "No man can become a true theologian by the perusal of works that are only theological," — a truth wonderfully in harmony with the principle of the text. And a careful meditation on that truth by us all, would be a great deal better, doubtless, than the sermon you will hear this morning. In its little mustard-seed is a glory that can fill all the heavens of life.

This truth applies not only to theologians and to religious teachers, but to all teachers and all subjects. Would a man be a philosopher? It won't do to begin and end with Aristotle, Plato, Descartes, or Kant. He must be not only of the sensational school, but must know the ideal school as well; and not stopping there, he must acquaint himself with the great sceptical school; mastering that, he will be ready to pass into the mystic order of thought; and thence finally on to the grand eclectic method, wherein he will stand balanced, master of what has been, candidate for what may be.

Would a man become proficient in science? He must remember that astronomy alone cannot make him so. Astronomy is dependent upon mathematics. The science of botany is full of beauty as well as use; but it is intimately connected with and dependent upon the science of chemistry. The birds of the air, the beasts of the field, and the fishes of the sea, subsist upon the great economy of organized matter. If you would understand the vegetable kingdom, you must go down into the mineral kingdom, and catch the whispers through which the latter talks to the former, and understand somewhat the terms of amity through which they hold intercourse. The eye and the hand, the head and the foot, are not independent anywhere.

Are you an artist? You are not so because you can build a house, a barn or a temple. You are so, if at all, because you possess *art*,— or, rather, art possesses you. You must study this wonder in its fellowships. You will build a better house if you understand sculpture; and chisel better if you can paint; and sing better if you can do all the rest, whether in form, color, tone, thought or passion. You must know the great world of beauty in itself, and its laws as they stand related to the world of sense and the laws of expression. Then you can do anything that needs to be done.

The statesman is not such because he understands the labyrinths of diplomacy, or has his hobby in legislative halls or cabinets. He is so because he understands not only the constitution, the code and the policy of his own country, but because he is well versed and broadly read in the history of social organization and action. He must know monarchy, the genius of despotism, patriarchy, aristocracy, as well as democracy; all forms of government and how they came to be — the providential necessity of them.

The lawyer wants familiarity with not only his codes and precedents, and rules of evidence and pleading, but he needs also to know men, the code of motives, the internal statutes of equity, the constitution and precedents of human nature, together with long ranges of history and philosophy.

The physician must be skilful in physiology and the materia medica; he must be facile in diagnosis, prognosis, and clinics. But it won't do for him to stop there. He must be more comprehensive, or he will kill and cure by the same rule. He needs to know pathology of feeling and of thinking; he must be a detective of moral symptoms; he must have insight into the spiritual coloring and weather of the soul, and know how to modify and control this subtle sorcery of the sick-room, if he would be master of the issues of life and death.

And the preacher needs to be best furnished of all. If what is said of him be true, namely, that his themes are the highest, his responsibilities the greatest, then should he be most comprehensive and ample in his furnishing. He needs to be not only an "earthen vessel" but a fountain if possible; a theologian not only of the *azoic* period, but of the age of *living men;* not simply a mnemonic, a guant pilgrim with his basket full of relics and charms, but an inspired prophet with the whole counsel of God. He must know not only the technics of his sect-school, denomination and church, he must also know the minds and characters of men as they stand recorded in general history and general literature. He must know not only what he himself thinks, but what his neighbor thinks; and be as patient under *his* thought as under his own. He must know not only his specific religion, but, if he be a Christian, he must know all other religions. The true teacher must study them; he must find what truth there is in them; how they came to be, and to be when and what they were and are. He has no right to shut his eyes, and then stone the Mohammedan, or the Jew by whose Scriptures he also swears. He has no right to refuse to read by the light of the proximate noon of the West, the old religions of the East, in any of their diverse forms or powers, whether in Egypt, India, or Persia. The men there were and are his brothers, differing in their origin, constitution, and wants in no respect from himself. The differences are external, accidental, non-essential, and he cannot be a wise teacher who refuses to know the why and the wherefore of these things.

And the true theologian should be wide and luminous in the world of science as well as letters. Science is God's divine law in nature. His first Bible was not this, but that — two volumes on the same subject. They go together; and he who cannot accept this truth is no fit leader for the blind, or even for those who have vision. The theological teacher must be learned, so far as he can be, in the divinity of God's thoughts, wherever and however he has spoken them, whether in the Bible, creation, providence, or the human soul. If he would indite and perpetuate a theology that is worth anything, that will be remembered a day after he is done, he must give it no provincial accent, but make it speak in a language universal as God. Otherwise one had better be in counting-rooms, on commercial wharves, bridging oceans, building cities, wherein men do greatly and truly.

Indeed, it would be well if all preachers would study more of the divinity of actual life, know men and the world they live in. We all know at what a discount the pulpit stands in practical wisdom, a knowledge of affairs. We would hardly be trusted to draw a check, if we had the right. The world would not pick us out to manage railroads, engineer great commercial enterprises, solve problems of political economy, and make laws for the regulation of states and institutions. And yet we ought to know men in their life and action, because here their characters are made; motives and principles come into play; life comes to success or failure. For life lived and done in the body and the reasons thereof, and for nothing else, shall we be judged.

The minister and theologian should know the pathology of mind and heart in the concrete; what human sickness is in the moral and spiritual sense, and how it is to be cured. Charms, relics, mystic spells, medicine-men, rain-makers, cloud-compellers will not do it. The hurt of the mind and heart is to be healed by generating underneath the wound what is right and pure and true, till all be full of health. A preacher will preach a better sermon for having large secular knowledge, just as a shoemaker will make better shoes if he has studied anatomy for the balance and pose of the human form; just as a dressmaker will make a better fit and a better costume, on hygienic principles, if she has studied the physiology of her sex; or a blacksmith make a better bolt, knowing perfectly the expanding and contracting forces of heat and cold on iron. A laborer will sleep better in the night if he has earned a good conscience during the day, and understands ventilation and the electric currents of earth and atmosphere. A Christian will pray a great deal better if he has studied the value of pure air, and warm sunshine, and clean water, and good digestion — for prayers are not worth much that steam up out of the diseased results of violated law. They are not healthy. All things, all laws, all divine functions, go together — head, heart, hand — through and through the world.

These remarks are preliminary; and their value lies in the fact that they more easily raise, and give posture to, what is more especially my subject; which is, the notice of some of the leading characteristics and tendencies of modern thought. I will mention four: *Breadth, Consistency, Depth, Unity*.

First, *Breadth*. You cannot talk with a man five minutes — if he is the kind of man you like to talk with — without perceiving how his mind is shooting out in almost every direction, upon almost every subject; but especially on subjects related to his more immediate interest. He wants to know not only what he does know of the matter, but also what he does not know. He is under the inspiration of one of the great characteristics of modern intelligence, namely, the great truth, that all things are related. He does not know that which he assumes to know, until he understands the boundaries of it, what lies next to it, and determines it to be what it is. The moment a man feels the contagion of this expansiveness, has caught the grand sympathy of related truths, he begins to think truly; and thinks as never before. There comes at once more breadth and scope to him. Perhaps not more depth as well, but certainly more mental expansion; a wider perception of the working of all ideas and of the practical truths that men do know, than ever before. And it is this which makes more practical men, men of finer executive ability. Compared with a hundred years ago, one man can do the work of fifty, or of a thousand, simply because of this broadening, generalizing and systematizing tendency and order of thinking. This touching of the conjunction-points among related ideas, is the seed of all mental enlargement.

Secondly, this is a day in which men not only see truth in its relations, but also in its *correlations*, how one truth is fraternal and necessary to another. They begin to see as never before that ideas go in pairs; that they go in families. There is parent and offspring, brother and sister. Ideas go in communities. A whole colony of truths will sometimes leap into a man's mind like inspiration, simply because he is in this atmosphere, or the life of this law; not only of the relations of things, but of their correlations, their fellowship, their mutuality. That kind of thought is very marked in the thinking world to-day; it rules men of science; it governs the true interpreter of God anywhere and everywhere.

In the third place, notwithstanding the superficiality of the world, men are to-day more *radical* than ever. They go more to the root of things; send down into the darkness peering questions, that do not come back until they bring answers. What men want to know is, the foundations of things; the unquestioned certitudes in which this truth or that idea stands; the very root and principle of things. Men are asking such questions as never before; and that is one reason why they do not stop at phenomena, declining to accept as finality the mere sign or signal thrown up as a provisional expediency for a time. They must go deeper, are not willing to rest as rational beings, until they have touched the root of the matter. A *true* radicalism is one of the finest signs of the times; a radicalism which is born of the brain, not of the stomach or the liver; an instinct for truth, audacious, veracious, persistent, finely mannered, finely balanced; which sings and paints and aspires, but never scoffs, never pulls down, never uproots. If it chance to come upon some old snag of error, it will be less apt to raise issue with *it*, than to plant a seed of truth still deeper, and cultivate that till the new supersede the old and take possession of the field. In the divine order, evil is always overcome by good.

Finally, *Unity*. The yearning of men to-day is unspeakable for this. Wherever it finds a truth, here or there, whether it be a blooming thing of beauty for the hour, a glowing, throbbing pulse in the sky, or a hieroglyphic down deep in the earth, anywhere, everywhere, the great yearning restless asking is, How do these stand related? What is their common origin? How do they all consist, and what is the high point of view from which the whole is seen as one grand, beautiful harmony? Some men say, there is a God from whose standpoint all this may be beheld, and from whom the whole conception sprang.

Others say the plan originated itself. But the great truth stands, in any case, of this related order and harmony of things. This oneness which the mind and heart yearn for, is an inborn instinct, a necessity of rational intelligence. To think it is to affirm it and obey it. Men will not accept anything in these days, until they see in an intelligent way how it stands in relation to, and in consistency with, this grand idea of integral wholeness. When that is seen, the new truth is welcomed as a brother from the same home and parentage. Men give it their right hand heartily.

Breadth, Consistency, Depth, Unity; these are characteristics and tendencies of all live thinking to-day.

And yet, divine as all this evidently is, there are always some to break faith with it. Let a truth of nature be introduced to a truth in religion, a truth learned from the flower be put alongside a truth learned from this Book, and their harmony, fellowship and brotherhood be spoken of as of children of the same Father, and not a few are disturbed, possibly alarmed. Religion seems contradicted, imperiled, profaned. The reason is, they have never thought broadly; they have not been in the habit of contemplating ideas in their relations to each other. They are somehow under the sway of old falsehoods, that matter is evil, that nature and the world generally belong to the Devil because they are his work. Whereas, when they find out the truth, all these are as divine as the Maker that actually made them. All are one, and for one grand end working together. When our faith takes the truth in, our faith is increased. When our prayers sweep this scale, they not only bring us nearer to God, but send pulsations through all the life of heaven. When our faith stretches out to the extent that it may gather in *all* truth, then we shall begin to live a true religious life. So far as faith and truth are concerned, we begin to be saved. Then, enthroning God over all, because He made all and is in all, enfolding all, we shall not be terrified even if we overhear prayers from bending ones before the great Altar of the skies, from worshipers hidden away in the inner cloisters of Nature herself, from the mute but reverent lip of all things. On the contrary, we shall be anxious to combine their fervor and inspiration with our own, and chime all such vibrations of truth into accordance with our own wants and aspirations.

Nowhere do these truths apply more fully than to religion of course. The characteristics and tendencies of thought to-day have consciously more to do with religion than any other one subject. The whole Christian man is not only anxious to know, and to carry out his own personal convictions, but he is interested that his neighbor shall also do the same. But because he has gotten the grand idea of this related fellowship of all truth, he does not expect to be damaged by the success of his neighbor's thought; he expects rather to be lifted and supplemented thereby. He is never troubled because there is another denomination in the world, another churchfold of different name from his own, or a different way of theological thinking. He rejoices therein.

And yet there are thousands withering and shrivelling up to-day because, forsooth, they think it wrong to go out of Judea and the Bible for God. Somehow or other they stick in the letter and bark of Christianity, regardless of root or fruit. Many are there of this kind. Nevertheless, it stands true that all through the world, ever since man existed, God has never been without his witnesses, never been without his worshipers. The Christian's business, especially if he be a Christian teacher, is, to study not only Christianity in denominations and in history, but to study the *religious nature of man;* to study that mighty sentiment, that wondrous function in human nature, as it has manifested itself *all through time.* If I, as a teacher, am not ready to do that, I had better be doing something else. In place of bringing before you the obsolete refrains of things that have had their day, won their victories, and gone to their urns and epitaphs, — of glory, if you please, we must strike for breadth and advancement, letting our thoughts go out fraternally everywhere, to every brother.

And we must not say that he is not our brother, because he is of a different latitude and longitude; of a different religion, worshiping a different *external* God. Do we not all know that we make our own God, every one of us? The Ethiopian makes his black; the Greek makes his beautiful and sensuous; the Egyptian made his of stone and night. Every man makes his God according to himself. He issues a high edition of himself — I am speaking of his conception of God, of course. When shall we learn that these *conceptions* are not God himself—dissolving, melting away, behind which is the one everlasting true God, coming out more and more into revelation, just like the hidden statue in the marble. From the first day's chipping you would not know what the block was to be, even as you would not know the Christian God through the wooden, stone and iron devices of Him among other nations and ages.

But the true God is coming out through light, through reason, through intelligence, through virtue, more and more. And I don't want to stop Him; I don't propose to arrest this coming of a better conception of God into the human soul, saying thus far and no farther. Though it might be easier to get along with religion by taking it for granted that God is known as much as He can be, and religion is all finished at our hands, we having nothing to do but to believe it. Still the assumption would be fatal. The theologian, the religious teacher now, must flavor what he knows from the universal scale of what can be known. He will be better furnished for his work through the teaching and culture of general literature, than by gathering all he can get from the technicalities, special schools and theologies of men, and staying shut up there.

What religious teachers, and religious pupils — what men of all classes and positions to-day want, is broad, general life-culture. The Christian now should be broadly read, broadly-thoughted; he cannot live on the same catechism that once served him; he cannot live on the same creed forever. Neither borrowed thought nor the signs of thought can bring him thrift; he must break away and think for himself; must harness himself up in fundamental, universal principles, and live in the inspired consciousness of the essential harmony and divine unity of all truth.

Then he will be balanced; there will be no danger of his becoming a fanatic; the more radical he is, the more truly conservative will he be. In a word, religion, whether as existing in the simple, sweet graces of virtue and character, or the heavier statements of theological thought, will be a living power. Toward such a power the tendencies are stronger to-day than ever.

A Christian cannot pass off his professions for his character as once he could. He does not stand at a premium for any public or private trust where capacity and integrity are required, simply because he is the member of a church. He ought to. And I trust there is to be a new departure in this matter. I want to see the time, and it should be right here now, when the fact that a man professes to preach the Gospel, or belong to a Gospel church or a Gospel congregation, will be a certificate that he will not tell an untruth; that he will not cheat; that he will not steal his neighbor's gold or reputation; that he will not plaster himself all over with the commandments of Christ, and then violate their spirit from sun to sun. It is a broad satire, even now, for Christians to prove their orthodoxy by saying, "I do not trust to good works for my salvation; salvation is a matter to be looked after by another." Such testimony is usually superfluous. But the time will come when such a confession of faith will be classed with holy water and the blood of bulls.

What men need now is to be right and truthful; in sympathy with God wherever He has spoken or made a sign of Himself; arrayed in a panoply of everlasting truth, beauty, purity and blessedness. Does a man really live? What is he to do with his life? If he die shall he live again? These are great questions; none greater. For the life to come will take care of itself; it is nothing but the blossoming of the seed we plant here. Our anxiety is to be all here.

There is a special significance in such thoughts, from the fact that to-day there is a mingling of all nations, religions, peoples and races of the earth, as never before. In this broad commingling and fellowship we need to have keen insight, the detective faculty, to discern what truth they all have. Old walls are broken down; restrictions are removed; and there is a mighty rush of life, a mighty intermingling of diversities; and there is no way of harmonizing them but by striking for the *universal* truth that underlies all life, and holding to that as the orchestra holds to the key. Accidents, provincialisms, mere local and temporal matters, are to go for nothing.

And this is especially true of our own country.

Just look at our immediate community. There would not be a man of us alive to-day, if the old authorized plan were acted upon, namely, of burning a man for differing in opinion from another. But thanks to improvement, that is not sound doctrine now. Religious thought in our day is asserting and maintaining true liberty. Theology is enlarging so as to include all related truths of science. If Christianity is to lead the world, she must drop her old provincialisms; she must drop her old "shibboleths," and stand on her everlasting, fundamental, universal principles. She is to shake out each wrinkled fold of her great banner, and let every stripe and star flash in the sun. He who refuses all this, does not comprehend the spirit of Christianity or his day. The spirit of Christianity holds just this breadth, depth, harmony, and oneness. Its spirit, I say, not its letter; not its external history; not its phenomena. Those things are fleeting, temporal; they are dead; they die in their birth, many of them.

A Christian church in the better day to come, will be something more than an organized enterprise to extend the church-roll of membership, or to secure an affluent exchequer for charity and other disbursements. The bankers, merchants, the social and fraternal guilds, will beat us out and out in such matters. As to things instrumental and accidental to a good, vigorous, working policy, we all understand that. They are a power and necessity in their place. But they are only the coal and the ropes and the rigging on board the ships, and not the ships themselves, nor their cargoes, nor their destinations. If we think differently, we shall only decay at the wharf, however splendidly appointed.

The church has a great work to do in this day. It was very easy once to run over a list of articles and subscribe to them; to recite a catechism; to observe one day in seven according to set usages. But the work of the Church to-day is the rearing of the grandest civilization possible; the rearing of the grandest humanity conceivable; subsidizing, in this glorious endeavor, every truth available in the universe. When this work is truly accepted, we shall hear no more whining about evolution, or development, or atheism. When the manhood of faith comes, the measles of the cradle won't trouble anybody. Should not a church, a pulpit, a theology, stand in the very van of progress and of thought in any and every hour of the world? Should it not lead, sounding the trumpet of advance, the bugle-blast, *onward?* charging over hill and valley, instead of following in the rear with the ambulances, the vials of odors, and the therapeutic skill and industry of the ages? Is religion nothing but a hospital, fit only for invalids and imbeciles? Is it nothing but a school of surgery and medicine? We can treat it so if we please; but as we treat it so *we* shall be. If the half or the tithe of what we have hinted be true, shall Christianity be represented as divorcing religion from life and the laws of the universe, and then be permitted to boast that she is the only true religion? and that by and *for* her Christ, were *all things* made, and in Him do *all things* consist? Should we not show our faith by our works?

Let us not be behind, then. Let us cultivate executive skill. Let us seek to attain grand consistency in this work of life. The Church should be the university for manhood, and the university for womanhood, with life for the tuition time, and success or failure for graduation. Looking upward, let us bring into relation all fraternal truths, in nature, in providence, in the world of beauty; let us harmonize all these correlative fellowships; let us strike for the root of things; and over all enthrone one Creator, one grand intelligent order of infinite, sympathetic thought. Then all shall act in living, harmonious concurrence, and life and strength and virtue will be the result. Religion shall be to us a perpetual inspiration, making us better and nobler; more affluent in all that is true, beautiful, and good. The soul shall grasp the living truth; it shall put things fitly together by their joints, in every part; and thus it shall divinize itself in truth, in life and love, not only here, but forever.

And this is my theme this morning: the tendencies and characteristics of the thinking world to-day, more potent in religion than anywhere else, for truth, goodness, and joy. Let us accept the hand of God as He extends it in providence. Going to the front, let us hearken for the word of command and advance. "Great and marvelous are thy works, Lord God Almighty; just and true are thy ways, thou King of saints."

Be this the song and the inspiration of our pilgrim march.

VIII.

FEAR AND LOVE.

> *The fear of the Lord is the beginning of wisdom.* — Psalms iii. 10.
> *Perfect love casteth out fear.* — John i. 4, 18.

THE Old and the New dispensations put together. Fear first: The death of fear and triumph of love at last.

Fear begins the lesson of wisdom; that is all. It does not continue it. After the initial step, it has no place. As man grows wise, cowardice drops out. The seed that was planted in the night and frost of trembling, appears in the blossom of love and the fruit of worship.

The ground of fear in religion is threefold: *instinct; wrong ideas of God;* and a *wrong condition in man.*

The child trembles in the dark. He is finite, weak, and immature. The child uses no such words; he is conscious of no such meanings; but instinctively the shadows of dread are born in him and *seem* to hover about him.

Wrong conceptions of God fill men with terror. They make bondmen of them, slaves, servile captives as if chained to some royal car to grace the conqueror's triumph. In this sense God is thought of as omnipotent, indeed, but *arbitrary*, having a greater care and jealousy for his own rights and glory than for the good of his children. And these wrong conceptions of God as a magnified Jupiter, make men afraid of Him, even grown men.

And then again these terrors are bred in the nest of evil and wrong in man's nature. Nothing will make men such cowards as conscious guilt; nothing will take the stability out of a man's knees, or his heart, or his eyes, like an accusation from home. The very leaf whispers in demon voice; the sweet fragrance of flowers is the disguised breath of some enemy near in the dark.

And so for this threefold reason men are in fear; and fear is their master.

This fear, especially religious fear — for of that I am speaking this morning — has wrought all manner of direful works in the world. Their name is legion — Moloch, Satan, Calumny, Sacrilege, Deceit, Guile, Extinction of Light, Confiscation of Honor, Blight of Manhood, Famine of Soul, Death and Disaster of all spiritual Hope and Power. No people ever rose from the inspiration of fear. No nation ever attained height and power and honor from the stimulation of that genius. No pure religion ever flourished in its shadow. No noble character was ever created by such motive, or the forces generated by it. Fear makes man ignoble. Instead of weaving crowns, it discrowns him. Making never a hero, it dooms possible heroism often to cowardice and craven meanness. No God was ever truly worshiped, with fear as an inspirer. No God was ever loved who was dreaded. Bad as man is, he is not about to seek such embraces. No wonder the instinct of selfishness under the name of religion, has forced and bribed man to buy himself off from the power and purpose of an Omnipotence he dreaded, counting it his highest possible fortune to get out of his hands at whatever price.

Fear, as a religion, makes God mercenary and man venal. As men have risen in intelligence, in virtue, in civilization, in conquest over the world God bade them subdue, fear has dropped out; the vassal has disappeared; bondage has become more and more a name without meaning. To rise, to be truly exalted, is to become free — freemen under God, not his slaves. Nations have always gone up as their ideas of religion have risen. The grade and character of the religion of a people constitute its social thermometer. You can read the altitude of humanity on the scale of its faith, whether pertaining to communities, nations, families or individuals. Joy, purity, liberty, light, worship, have blossomed out from human nature under the liberating and fructifying touch of light and love; and so far as this order of things has come, salvation has come.

So that religion is a graded order of *education;* the unfolding, fructification, and elevation of man's nature in relation to God's nature; the opening of his eyes to see who his Father is, and what; and such internal condition as receives and develops the character of God himself. Beginning in fear, its education passes up out of fear, by a regular grade, through intelligence, and culminates in love.

Intelligence is necessary. Not one step out of the night and degradation of superstition has the world ever moved, save as lifted by intelligence — emancipation of the mind from ignorance by means of truth. The great world of law, order, science, has done immensely already to break up the empire of superstition. She has slackened her grasp not once upon human nature, save as it has been neutralized by the touch of truth and reason.

But that is not enough. Intelligence even of angelic ken and flame, must be *impregnated* by a life and a quality from *above itself*, or some hour will come when its own results will fall back upon itself like ashes from spent fires. It must be so, or there is no immortality for its functions; no God related to man. In a word, it must be so, or we are talking like insane men about religion this morning.

But that culminating stage is designated by the word *love;* passion of the heart; century flower of nature's toil; the last slumbering possibility in humanity evoked and matured by the summer glow of *God's* love. We love him because he first loved us. We touch God, doubtless, by instinct, primarily. But He meant to get the world out of that as soon as He could. Then we touch Him through the world itself, through nature, creation, providence, the vast realm of intellectual life and power where God thinks and his glories flame out. We call it law sometimes, and science at others. This world of law, science and reason, as the manifestation of God, should not alarm professors and teachers of religion, when spoken of in connection with worship and faith. God's thoughts and ways will not hurt anybody's piety in this world, or prospects for the next.

But God comes to us, also, through the Scriptures; He speaks through Prophets — the grand seers of time, the teachers and revealers — personally of his own personality. God comes especially near to the heart of the world, its love-organ, in that He drops his own love by a Divine word or syllable, out of his own heart, into this very love-capacity of our nature. Here, in this last communication, we seem to get a more radical hint of the fatherhood of God, than anywhere else — our Father as well as Creator — care-taker. Well may it be said that "He *first* loved us." Did you ever know a monstrous parent? Then you knew one without love; and God without that paternal attribute may be well feared, dreaded and deprecated as monstrous. Why, the world would give another god, if it could command Him, to get itself out of his hands and out of his power. I don't wonder at the theology of fear — dark, bloody, fallen! It is the eclipse of God and the night of Paganism. How it has *coarsened* the world and brutalized it!

This graded order of Christian education, starting from the night of fear, flashing on from the realm of intelligence, until the height at last be touched of love, purity, and worship, stands confirmed by history.

Go back to the old religions; go back among the Pagan gods and faiths, and what do we find? Is man at his best estate in religion back there? Is the prospect more cheering as you retreat? Any room for improvement, think you? The lowest and most primitive form is that of Fetichism, where men have their fetich-god, a mere creeping thing, inanimate, disgusting often. There is fear there — *nothing else*.

Then passing up from that, you find men having gods tidy enough, because made of brass, silver, fragrant wood, shrines, pictures, sylphs, and shining demons. But the end is not there. We find religion pronouncing itself in still higher forms by and by, the forms of abstraction, ideal conceptions, imagination; some of them beautiful creations; some of them deformed and direful; all aglow with human passion; finely tinted with prophetic light, many of them. These stages of religion you find back among the old classic and cultivated nations and peoples of antiquity.

Finally, religion comes up to the Fatherhood of God and the Brotherhood of Man. " Love the Lord thy God with all thy heart, and thy neighbor as thyself." Not fear now, but reason, love, and a sound mind reign; not stocks and stones; not dreamy abstractions, but love, born from one being's nature, toward the nature of another being; a heart-flame kindled in the lower by the pregnant touch of the higher. A perfect religion casteth out all fear, all bondage, all servility, through the dominion of perfect love.

I intimated a moment ago that many suppose there is no such thing as improvement in religion.

Improvement in commerce, the arts, governments, money-making, and so on; but no improvement in religion! Alas! Is the Sermon on the Mount no improvement upon doves and bullocks, children in the Ganges and mud-turtles of the Nile?

Go back over the world and begin down in the night of fear where the crocodile is God, and man trails his devotion in the slime-path of the reptile. Follow up the idea of religion as man had it then, and has it now, and will have it by and by; and then babble no more about the ancient way as better than those the latter days cast up. The history of man is the history of improvement. A graded order of religion, science, civilization, manhood, from the cradle to the grave, is the Divine economy; and truth is more revealed to-day than ever.

But where do we stand, personally? It is easy to preach about this, and hear about it; and if we agree to be satisfied all round, we are apt to think the Lord's work is done. And yet the question is not superfluous: Where do we stand in this matter of religion? In bondage or out of it? building on hell and her shadows, or on heaven and her heart eternal? drawing the inspiration of our motives from the Devil and his interests, or from God and his nature? Fear hath torments; fear hath hell; fear hath bondage. I hope I am positive enough to be understood. We carry within us the material out of which all moral futurity is made. Fear drives people away from religion — no joy in it. They think, without saying it a great many times: "Religion is painful;

it is a yoke; it has something grindingly irksome about it; and when I want a good time I go elsewhere for it." Why is it irksome? Why, churches are regarded as a sort of vaccination institution, which the world would have nothing to do with if possible. Whereas, the true idea of a Christian Church is not that; its meaning is the almoner of God's life-bread to the world; it should be the grand inspiring tuitional school that feeds a man and lifts his nature to beauty, purity and glory, though there were no such possibility as perdition, or disease of sin in the universe. We break religion in two, and take the selfish half and call it "the mercy of God to us miserable sinners." The greatest sin we ever commit is this infraction of the Divine integrity, for we violate our own integrity in doing it. Churches ought to be the most attractive places in the world, vastly more so than the theatre or banqueting-hall. And they would be if rightly administered. They would be if men had the right conception of God, and of a human soul, and that soul were up to the development of the spiritual sense, and the joy capacity, and open to the highest inspiration in the universe.

It is perfectly right and divine for a man to live from day to day by a morsel of bread. You never hear me fling disparagement upon the good things of this world, upon the fading beauties of the hour even, the joyous glee of children, the royal day of manhood. But man does not live by *bread alone.* I am talking of his relation to God, on the supposition that if he die he shall live again. A great many times men have not anything at home to be religiously interested in; their development is small, or lies in other directions; their tastes are cultivated on other objects — right enough in their place, but they are not the whole of man; they mark not his higher, noblest opportunity. If there is anything in religion, anything of truth in God — this is the great matter of existence. Churches are for men, in the highest, truest sense. We want right conceptions of God, right conceptions of the human soul, and a right idea of human life — what they are for, these passing days of opportunity and duty.

Look back, then. The further we go, the more positively we strike into the religion of fear. The present handles religion on the arena of intelligence greatly, a conflict of ideas. The religion of the future will come out in the victory of LOVE, wherein heart and brain shall be winner; and of the offspring thereof there shall be no end. Much of the theology of the past holds no thinking man or woman to-day; and you know we always mean by theology, what men think, what they guess, what they quarrel about. Religion is a different matter. The present contest about theology is this: on one side, whether God is nothing *but* reason; and on the other, whether there is any reasonable God *at all;* reason with no God, or a God that is rational. That is the battle of mind. The future will crown both the God and the reason; the nuptials will be recelebrated of a wicked divorce which man, in his short-sightedness and in his darkness of fear and error has caused. The fire of the higher nature shall kindle the fuel of the lower, and the flame shall be worship immortal. Then the new heavens and the new earth will appear, and there shall be salvation.

Get worthy conceptions of God, then; obtain worthy conceptions of man; seek for right conceptions of human life; and especially, if possible to specialize, fire yourself with a right and powerful conception of what it is possible for you *to be*. Growth in wisdom is the great business of life and religion; growth in the wisdom of the text is the path to heaven. To know God rightly is inevitably to confide in Him — that is faith. To be won by God is just to answer back from our love unto the love that He gave, first loving us. That love is worship. Therein is salvation.

Let me repeat: fear hath torments; he that feareth is not made perfect; perfect love casteth out fear. More and more is your love casting out fear, if you have the true kind; and at last fear will have perished.

When the fruit is ripe, the fairest blossom must fall; the rough spring winds are all over, and the gathering time is at hand. When the Zion of humanity shall sing, as she certainly will sing, that will be the time in which her bondage and her dark trepidations shall have ended.

Only two more thoughts. First, have such conception of your God as shall win your love of Him, or you cannot love Him; secondly, live such a life yourself as not to be afraid of Him, or you cannot worship Him. Gather right and inspiring ideas of his character, then make your own character conform to that.

Thus you will build not on hell, but on the foundations of heaven; and the gates of darkness and disaster shall not prevail against you.

IX.

THE WORTH OF THE SOUL AND ITS APPROPRIATE TREATMENT.

> *What is a man profited if he shall gain the whole world and lose his own soul? or what shall a man give in exchange for his soul?* — Matthew xvi. 26.

THESE are great words. They throb with unspeakable meaning. Evidently they are great in that they come home directly to the main question of religion, of life, of man.

The value of the soul is taken up here. A proposition handling its worth is thrown upon our thought. The implication is, there can be no perfect equation where the soul is one member. "Though a man gain the whole world," which means everything, "and lose his soul," where is his profit? The silent answering must be, nothing; nay, more, he is defrauded.

Men get the eye open sometimes afterward instead of beforehand; and the backward look is not half so profitable as the foresight would have been. So the question comes up, What would a man give to regain his soul? for that is the spirit of the question. What would he not give? puts it more forcibly. Alas! what can he give, if, possessing all things, that is but a mote in the balance of its value? The soul is beyond price. I take it as we have it. I know that is not the exact literal form of the question. Throwing it into the optative mood, giving man the choice, possibly the strict thought is, Has man anything left which he can add to the price he sold his soul for?

Three thoughts here come practically upon the mind: First, salvation is a work; secondly, a work on and for the soul; thirdly, it consists of what we make of the soul by that work. The logic you will see in the next verse; for, says the great Teacher, "The son of man shall come, and then he shall reward every man according to his works." What, says one, are works a foundation on which to build the rewards of heaven? Just read the verse again: "The son of man shall come in the glory of his Father, and then he shall reward every man according to his *works*." Such was Christ's opinion, at least.

Put in a single sentence, the truth is thus: *The soul is saved so far as it is treated according to the doctrine of its nature and necessities.*

The Christian world is changing front. Instead of facing, as for the centuries, toward cloisters, and monasteries, and castles, and cobwebs glittering in the sky, Christianity is fronting toward man, toward life, toward humanity or the soul. Faith and intelligence are turning their back upon the former things of man, while in doing that we come face foremost to the first things of God.

Hence the modern drift of thought. The thinking we get now, somehow or other, right or wrong, is toward the humanitarian point. This drift is toward *fact* instead of *speculation;* more toward psychology than theology; for theology man makes, while psychology God makes. As time goes on the mind grinds itself down deeper and deeper, and more and more directly on to the hard pan of truth and fact in place of speculation; of science or certainty, rather than guess or mere hypothesis, waxing and advancing continually, while the counterview which grounds in mere opinion, is waning. Everything in every way is tending and drifting toward the practical and actual, and away from the speculative and hypothetical. I cannot stop it, you cannot stop it. Wisdom would seek rather to gather up the reins and guide the movement, than find fault and block the wheels of the advancing chariot.

Salvation, then — if we go by the New Testament and its spirit — means the soul evolved, developed, educated, cultivated, grown, ripened and perfected. Final maturity is the saved state. The method thereof and thereto is the *way* of salvation.

This means the growth and the maturity of every department of our being. If you leave out any one, of course, there is trouble. I have no quarrel with men who contend that mere development or evolution alone is not religion. But, including the whole of man's being, what have they to say? The development of his intelligent nature, the development of his moral nature, the development of his spiritual nature, the development of every power, faculty, function and capacity in him, touching this life and the life to come, touching himself and touching his

Maker, waking up the entire man under divine inspiration, whether in this Book or any book, out of the heavens or out of the earth — what have we to object? All grand, all potent inspirations and stimulations are for the sake of piercing and penetrating this very normal acorn of being, with reference to unfolding it and bringing it to final oakhood — the germ to the finished crown of glory.

You will notice — for I hear the footfall of your whispering criticism — all this must be by *proper methods*. You may develop man's being as a whole, or in the line of some specific faculty or function. For instance, put man into a university, and you develop him intellectually, leaving all the rest. Put him into a school of art, and you develop him æsthetically; if you leave him there you save but a fragment of him. Develop him morally, and you may do it grandly, strongly, truly, as to that particular department of his being; but if it has no alliances, no intelligence, no purpose, no sentiment, all your morality will be a limping, deformed and fettered thing, a dwarf, a monstrosity. You sometimes find a man all conscience, nothing else; therefore no conscience at all that has any practical worth in it. Developed in the proper method, however, and matured according to that, salvation results and consists in that maturity.

I mean by this *method*, of course, a grand sketch and economy of culture, born in the conception of a Being *vastly superior* to the being to be educated. I mean a method of training and development sketched on a scale as broad as all the *outlying possibilities* of man's nature; and when you have that, you have the scale of his creation, which is the scale of his redemption, his immortality, his spirituality, his goodness, his salvation. Man trained and grown under these high conceptions, inspirations and methods, will unfold symmetrically. All there is in him will be challenged forth, and gathered up — will be saved instead of being wasted or lost.

That is the idea of salvation. No other scheme of religion ever spoke of it so fully and distinctly as the Christian; and because of this superiority of the Christian religion, it has this universality in it. It is adequate, exhaustive.

Thus we cannot but perceive the *image of God* which sleeps in us. This type of God — for we are his children — is just starting in us like a waking dream, a shadow passing more and more into substance through training and maturity. At last we shall be like God. Why not? If the child is true, and reaches the term stipulated for in its parentage, will it not be like the parent? But you are startled, perhaps, that I make man *like God;* and you say, we shall be lesser gods. Certainly; nothing startling in that. The startling thought is that we should fall short of that; that we should lack the certificate of our original at last; that we should go up maimed and half finished, bereaved, and somehow lacking in some grand feature or main element in completion. The difference between you and your Maker is to be a difference of degree. He is *infinite*, you are *finite;*

He is *Life itself*, you are a *recipient* of life from Him; you bear his image for that very reason. You are but a spark struck off here to be kindled into a flame of glory. You are a dark unconscious image or outline, to be awakened into a fact divine. So we hesitate not to speak of Godliness or God-likeness as pertaining to man. The whole problem of Christianity in connection with our souls is just this, that God should *reproduce Himself* in us; finite as He is infinite; pure as He is pure; holy as He is holy; blessed as He is blessed. When crowned in character with the fullness and sweetness of his love, then we shall be finished. Perfecting the soul in that way, *saves it*.

Here, then, we come into the new Kingdom, the kingdom of spirit. Who knoweth the things of man but the spirit that is in man? was inquired last Sunday. The spiritual Kingdom is *man's spirit spiritualized by God's spirit*. This sleeping image and dream of being smitten by the fire of inspiration from God's own life, is that which swells and expands and grows and bursts forth at last, throwing out leaf and branch, and bloom and fruitage divine. This is the kingdom of souls, minds, constellated thoughts, virtues and graces, and beatitudes unspeakable.

Right here in this interest comes in the *church*. The church is to be a kingdom-builder. She is to be an industrial organization for spiritual edification, the function of truth; in this way rearing up, educating, developing man's nature, waking up thought, the deep slumber of glory and immortality in us.

That is the only sense in which the church is a salvation provision. It is an educational force that is to act as God's summer acts upon the seed in the ground. It is to work as any tuitional power works upon undeveloped, raw, uneducated material.

Out of this idea, viz., soul development, the saving of the soul, flows the intellectual culture of the world. Read the history of the world and you will find that the pathway thereof is starred by triumphs, just in proportion as Christian inspiration has been permitted to touch the intellect and life. Science is born, laws are enacted, civil society is organized in strength, beauty, and purity, just in proportion as these higher methods of development and education seize the living spirit of man, his whole nature, and handle that nature according to its laws.

And there is no civilization on earth that will stay, save that which flows from just this fountain. True civilization is nothing but the spirit of man developed, purified, adorned, and enthroned over his material and sensuous circumstances. Men talk of ships and universities; they speak of commerce and material thrift, and all that, as constituting civilization. But eliminate this element named — the spiritual force in man, led to its possibilities by a spirit higher than itself — and the whole idea collapses, as history tells you, and man is a failure.

Let us come, then, by way of illustration, a little nearer to the practical line of our thought. Man is in darkness by nature; we understand that. Life is in darkness. O, how the old wisdom shrieked out for answers to the great questions which nothing but new morning-light was adequate to furnish! Religion is the *light* to dispel the darkness; a light in which man sees himself; a light in which he is to see his way, knowing one thing from another. Suppose a man turn his eye away from the abyss, and from the pathway, and gaze at nothing but light; peer into the sun; spend his grand hour of opportunity in speculation about the constituent elements of the luminous orb, how they have come together to constitute the sun; how rays act on vision, their chemical properties, mechanical and vital. Suppose he spend his time analyzing the beauties of light, and writing down tables giving statements in books of what he has discovered, or thought, or guessed, or imagined, as to the constituency of light, or its powers, what it can do, or be, or what it was designed to do. Why, the poor organ of vision itself would be dazzled to blindness, while the man would be left to tread his way in darkness. He would be just as liable to go wrong as right. Christendom has been full of star-gazers, sun-gazers; full of speculative, analytic faith on light, and what light has done and should do. Should you never look at the sun at all, if you knew nothing of its constitution, you could use the sun for what it shines for, namely, the discernment of objects revealed thereby. And the great object revealed by religion to you and me is, our nature, the soul, and the course it has to take to reach its glorious end.

There came a time once, and shortly after the

advent of Christianity, when the mind was actually blinded in this way. Very soon the Christian fathers were so wrapped in lunar speculations, or stellar calculations, or solar computations, as to the high sky of religion, that they forgot man. The poor thing called the soul, was in darkness; and the cold, damp cavern in which it lay, bred worms that crawled over it and gnawed away its life. Corruption rioted there while the teachers of religion were star-gazing, and giving new tabular arrangements and formulated statements of the constituents of things beyond the clouds. Then faith was all; the mind must believe so and so, as they wrote it, or be damned; while the poor soul was rotting in the damnation of falseness and neglect! If the light in such wisdom be darkness, how great is that darkness!

Religion is a *life* as well as a light. The beam has warmth in it, the shining ray is full of fire. The sun of nature in God's economy was designed to make the summer for the earth. Suppose a farmer to go forth and say, I am a husbandman; I can do nothing. The summer is all, and works are nothing with me. So he gazes at the sun, and believes in the sun; he goes to his books which wise men have written about the sun, the velocity of light, the intensity of heat, the luminousness of the ray, and what is in the sun and around it, and says: Every word of it *I believe*. *Credo, credo, credimus*. I believe; we all believe. But where is the corn? where is the wheat? where is the harvest of this believing husbandman? Had he never known anything of these speculative inquiries, the corn and the wheat would have grown; and true to his own powers and opportunities, his land would have yielded her abundant increase. So the faithful and obedient soul yields its resources, and grows and ripens into salvation.

There came a time once, when the world made just this mistake. Craft and convenience and greed of power came to religion and the Church, and said, Let us have a compromise. And the hand of the heavenly took the tainted hand of the earthly, and Christ and Cæsar were one. Old Constantine presided at the marriage of the priest of God and the priestess of the devil, and the nuptials are celebrated to this 'day. Doctors of divinity, doctors of law, teachers of churches spun fine cobwebs of divinity, so called, fine threads of speculation, and the proposition was: O church, O Divinity, if you will spin religion on these cloister spinning-wheels of speculation, we will run the man and the world; we will manage the soul and make the character. And it was agreed to. And down beneath the shadow of old cathedrals to-day lies rotting humanity, the price of that bargain. Religion was to believe things said, things taught by men. Religion must not have any work, any faith or scope in man's nature or in man's soul. Dead works, indeed! Which kind of works is best, think you, live works on live men, or dead works on dead speculations? One is forbidden by the Book, the other is enjoined to the extent that so far as you work out your own salvation in this life-work, you shall be saved. While cobwebs breed asthma, consumption and death, religion is a light, a life, a work on the soul, as we have affirmed it. The husbandry is there; the development there; the evolution there; moral, spiritual, beauteous, gracious; O how beautiful!

I was struck the other day by a grand thought just in this line, from one of the grandest essayists as well as historians in Europe. I will read it:

Many a hundred sermons have I heard in England; many a dissertation on the mysteries of faith, on the divine mission of the clergy, on apostolic succession, on bishops, and justification, and verbal inspiration, and the efficacy of the sacraments; but never during these thirty wonderful years, never one that I can recollect on common *honesty*, or those primitive commandments: Thou shalt not lie; Thou shalt not steal. All that Christianity was meant to do in making life pure, was left undone; while teachers gave themselves to spinning theological cobwebs.

Thus in place of the old material idolatry, we erect a new idolatry of words and phrases. Our duty is no longer to be true and honest and brave and self-denying and pure, but to be exact in our formulas; to hold accurately some nice proposition; to place damnation in straying a hair's breadth from some symbol which exults in being unintelligible, and salvation in the skill with which the mind can balance itself on some intellectual tight-rope.

So that all that Christianity was meant to do in making life pure and noble, is left undone; while teachers give themselves to spinning theological cobwebs and building speculative castles in the air.

Thus says the royal man. Brave words, indeed, to be spoken in Old England; but no braver than true.

This great matter we are all to look in the face.

The world has outlived the cobweb dynasty and economy. The cloister is drifting away into dim vistas, so far as it ever thought it meant man or God. The thought of the hour is coming directly to the *man*, and into man and his *nature*, into the grandeur of his neglected soul. Very early it was that Christendom sought a divorce of religion from morality — of what is *called* religion from actual manhood in life. This is the tendency always. It was and is the course of the whole heathen world. This very fact explains all religious revolutions, and many other revolutions, from the fact that that state of things is a falsity; the nature of man in its normal originality, being truer to God than any speculation of man on its abnormal wanderings; and it will invariably seek to rally and assert itself, when the falsity becomes so towering and so oppressive that it can be borne no longer.

Just look, in this country — I refer to the matter with perfect respect — look into the Episcopal Church to-day. What is the matter there? Why, Luther sleeps in human nature. The poor, mute, suppressed reformer is in the soul, and cannot brook delay much longer. How is it with old Catholic Europe? Grand conventions are organized; what for? The world has outlived the old speculations. The world has come to the conclusion that mere water effects no change whatever in character, whether it come down upon a man in a shower of heaven, or is applied at the tips of a bishop's fingers. A man is to be rewarded hereafter and here, at the tribunal of righteousness, according to his soul-work — according to what he makes of himself as a man in the ways of manhood, integrity, industry, and fidelity. Old Europe to-day recognizes that there is a bigger Luther in her at this very hour, than nailed the theses to the doorposts at Wittenberg. And you cannot stay these things. My admonition is: be not found in conflict with nature or Providence; but be men with eyes in front, and with ears listening Godward.

Now don't imagine that I have turned away from the gospel by turning to works which the gospel enjoins. Don't suppose we forsake God, and Christ, and Paul, and the evangelists, because we turn to the soul, and try to save it in the only way in which salvation has any intelligible meaning. We only turn from speculations, as you must see. The Gospel looks directly to man, to humanity, to the soul, or human nature. Don't be afraid of works. No soul is ever saved any further than it works out its own salvation, according to the God-inspiration working in it. The works we are warned against are the cobweb works, the ritual works, in such organization and institution of religion as is supposed to stand only to be believed. It is not faith in a machine that accomplishes anything; but the use of the machine — its application. Works of mercy — works of purity, gentleness, faith, honesty, manliness, womanliness, and of all the grandeur and beauty and splendor of all human capacities, are what the waiting hunger of God looks for. The stimulation, the growth, the ripening of all these, make the finished man. A cup of cold water given to a poor Chicago sufferer, is infinitely more divine and valuable in this matter of salvation, than all the theological cobhouses and monastic tapestries that were built or woven from the fourth century to the fourteenth. And you must know that right to those centuries we are often told we must go now for our doctrines and our creeds. Those great religious structures we are expected to look at, and to agree to believe; while as directly we are expected to neglect our own souls, and forget the nature God gave us. "Lord! Lord!" never saved anybody. Have we not believed this and that and the other? Cries never save. But the *doing* and *being* always save. *Do* those things and you shall never fall.

Man must be cultivated, then. He must be trained. His soul must be cared for. God has planted it here in the garden of time and opportunity. God's Church means responsibility and fidelity to the soul in its great culture. He has given the summer and the sunshine. He has pledged the dew and the air and everything. We must pledge industry. Thus we present our theme.

Think, then, O soul, what wealth sleeps within thee! What a grand thought it is: "I am a being in the image of God!" A mere conception of the possibilities that lie nascent within you, stirs aspiration and royal endeavor! Think what environment, what surroundings, what divine summer, what girding helpers, what flocking allies, from sky, from earth, from God, wait to lift and crown you! Think what divineness sleeps within thee, O soul, bearing the image of the Maker! What empty capacities, what waiting scope and scale of being to be filled out, to be realized by that fidelity which refuses to take any price for the soul, or itself! — which so handles the soul as to hold true to the estimate that Christ put upon it. It ceases, however, when it falls from its native scale, and is false to the injunctions of the opportunity of its birth.

Then think what a beautiful thing life is! How I rejoice in life every day, more and more! Think what a fine life every soul may live! Think what beautiful thoughts, what beautiful feelings, what grand sentiments, what high and glorious outlooks, we may come to be crowned with! Think what inspirations may lift us in the still morning hour, in the still night hour! Think what grand girdings of fellowship flock invisibly, inaudibly, around every soul that is true to itself, remembering its origin, remembering its destiny! Life, life! Think of it again, O ye who are flitting out of it, with souls swelling and bursting like spring buds, or withering and shrivelling and perishing like flowers broken from their stems!

Day comes out of night; so does the soul saved. Harvests ripen from spring seeds; so do souls under proper culture. The ore holds the precious metal which, when crushed, yields the pure diadem to sparkle forever; so does the soul under God. It has no equivalent out of itself, save God; and God who is its superior, not its equivalent, cannot come into commercial relations. God never sells Himself or his benefactions. No soul can find any substitute as an equivalent. Ideas of this sort breed confusion never set down in the Divine economy. There is no price for the soul. Not even Divinity stands in commercial relations to it.

The soul, to be saved by the Christian religion, must be *Christed* in character. The soul, to be saved by the religion of God, must be made like God in character. And when it is so changed, when it is so born again, there is wrought and certified in it the fitness of heaven. Heaven is its own palace; it becomes its own temple, its own mansion not made with hands, to be eternal in the heavens.

X.

SALVATION— THE OLD AND NEW VIEW.

What must I do to be saved? — Acts of
the Apostles xvi. 20.

IF you go into New York, or any of the great cities of the world, and seek to get a full and true view of any remarkable street, you will stand first on one side and look upon the other; then cross over and take the opposite position, and observe what confronts you there. Thus you get a complete view of the street.

So with thought. One-sided views are never whole views. In the midst of right and wrong, truth and error, we can never understand the right fully until we understand what is not right; we can never understand any truth or error so well as when we have contemplated, intelligently, the opposite of the truth or error.

I presented, last Sunday, what I believed to be the proper idea of *Gospel salvation*, viz.: *the truth which Christ taught, so applied to human life as to make man, in his life and character, Christ-like.* In other words, the soul educated, grown, ripened and perfected; the orderly and harmonious development of all our faculties; the growth and maturity of every department of our being — not omitting, of course, the due subjection and subordination of the selfish propensities of our nature. This final maturity, or this developed, well-balanced, well-ordered, Christ-like condition of the soul, is the saved state. And the method thereof is the *way* of salvation. This I said in my last Sunday's discourse.

But there is another view or theory; and it is old. I don't know of any doctrine much older, that has been ordained and authorized by the church, than this which I propose to set forth this morning. I am glad to have you know this other view. Indeed, you know it already. But, as I said at the outset, it is wonderfully instructive to contemplate opposites together.

The theory of salvation that we will state this morning, begins with the idea that man is lost in the *premises* of his nature; that in the fall of the supposed first man we all went down; and there we are, to begin with. It is assumed in the outset that we are sinners, condemned, and liable to the pains of hell forever; and the more dismal, abject and vile the picture we can make of ourselves, the nearer we are supposed to be to Divine truth on the subject. Thus all the world lies exposed to hell; and the refrain of most of the praying and believing of Christendom for the ages between us and the advent of Christ, has been a world, generation after generation, rolling on like billows over the sea to darkness and death. I don't wonder it has stirred the Christian heart to the very depths.

Accordingly, the first thing to be done in this way of salvation, is to become *convicted* of this terrible truth; not only somehow to know it, but to be *burdened* by a sense of it. The next thing is to get a conception, vitally in the mind and heart, that Christ died for us; in the first place as a substituted sufferer for our sufferings, as sin in place of our sin; that he took punishment in place of our punishment, and paid our debts. And in the second place, that by that death he has so appeased the wrath of God, and paid a certain penalty, that it *enabled* God to exercise forgiveness. When this conviction with regard to the lost condition of man, and with regard to Christ and what he has done, becomes so deep and influential as to become an experience, the believer is said to be *converted;* and the usual course is to confess it by joining the Church, and thus gain a putative standing among the saved. That is salvation — assumed to be salvation. Such a person is spoken of as in a hopeful condition, is regarded as among the children of God. That has been the faith of ages; and it is the faith of millions upon millions to-day.

Now, based upon this theory of salvation as to the doctrinal part of it, we find a corresponding theory of human life and the world. We all know how true it is that the world, under this view, is at once placed in contrast with religion; in opposition to religion; as its enemy, the enemy of souls, hostile and dangerous to salvation; so that the believer, or he who hopes for salvation on this ground, is admonished from the first against worldliness, against the vanity, pomp and ways of the world. He is admonished that his salvation is imperiled by conformity to the world. He is exhorted to forsake the world and flee from it; to avoid its pleasures, to separate himself from its interests, to drop its hot pursuits, and cultivate no longer its joys. He is urged and perpetually charged to abstain from worldly gratifications, as if it were dangerous even to desire fine houses, or extensive lands, to tread upon soft carpets, to sport rich and costly equipages and dress. Wealth is set forth as the most dangerous and subtle of all foes to the soul; so fearful is its influence for evil, that the impossibility of a rich man's entering heaven is symbolized by a camel going through a needle's eye.

The hopeful soul, under this theory of salvation, is warned from first to last against the vanity of *fashion;* he is never expected to be seen at the opera, or attending concerts; he is not to be borne about in beautiful carriages, possess costly paintings, travel, or even cultivate fine manners, lest he become not only worldly, but wander from the way of hope and life. The convert must never attend nor give parties; he must not enjoy any play or game; the dance is the unpardonable sin; and the charm of a stringed instrument, the devil's foremost.

This, you see, is the austere view of religion; it is the hard, horny way of being saved; it is the gloomy, joyless view. It is this view which makes children so dread the very name of religion. It is this view which makes them hate to go away from their plays, their sports and their young gush of joy which the flowers give them, and the music of streams and the glory of hills offer them, into the unattractive and joyless exercises of religion. They hate the unnaturalness of it. It is this fact which makes a great deal of religion irksome, not only to young life, but to mature life; this view it is which makes it seem so contrary to reason and common sense. The theory itself teaches religion to be against nature, the enemy of the material man, and the natural man the enemy of it. That is, to be natural is to be in danger of being lost. Hence the unnatural tone and manner, assumed a great many times, in which people talk about religion. They are artificial, unnatural, affected, disguised. So that it is very observable, upon a change of subject, how marked is the change of manner and tone. The face lights up like sunrise, and the voice rings like the chime of bells. They have got out of the irksomeness of religion into what is natural.

I will venture to say that nine out of ten of those here to-day have had this experience in childhood. They thought they must do and be so and so, and the more unhappy they were in their religion, the better the sign that they were in the right way. A conscientious child once justified his reading of a secular book on Sunday, by saying: "It makes me feel almost as bad as the Bible does." Under this view the reading of the believer is properly confined to a certain cast and range of thought. He must read, for instance, "Allein's Alarm;" "Edwards on the Affections;" "Baxter's Saints' Rest;" "Baxter's

Call;" and books of that sort, canonized and sanctified by the faith and piety of ages — for good men and women have believed this way.

I am only trying to state the doctrine, not judge it. Prayer, meditation, self-denial, self-contempt to a great extent, are supposed to be the process of grace and growth in knowledge and truth. So that our hymns, almost every one of them, are constructed on this basis of religion:

> "Look how we grovel here below,
> Fond of these earthly toys;
> Our souls can neither fly nor go
> To reach eternal joys."

No joy here. It is the refrain of a *lost cause!* Almost every hymn in this book is on that pitch. It is very difficult to find a hymn that rings out of a clear bell uncracked; the true voice of God, the angels' song that broke out upon the world when light and victory touched it. The refrain of a lost cause? No, never. Christianity is not the proclamation of defeat, but of a grand triumph. Almost all Christian prayers are deprecatory. Pick up any book of prayer of the last thousand or fifteen hundred years, and that is the key upon which they are pitched. So with extempore prayer — a piteous beseeching; a kind of lamentation over disaster and doom. The refrain is of the same kind in catechisms and confessions.

Now, all this is perfectly consistent. You cannot find in any book of logic a more consistent system of thought than this very view of salvation presents.

It is framed together and compacted in every joint and part. There are no loose joints. State the premises, and the conclusions are inevitable. The scheme hangs together. The lost condition of man— what Christ died for — hostility of the world to religion, and so on; it is all a consistent whole. To be consistent, the believer *ought* not only to quit the world and its follies, but its pursuits, its gathering of wealth, its dance of joy, its bloom of fields, its sheen of skies, its song of life. Secular! secular! is everywhere written. Dangerous! Beware! To be consistent he has no right to enjoy any pleasure, any pastime; scarcely may he smile. He has no right to follow the fashion.

O, believing man, believing woman, you break faith with yourself, and deny the force of what you write in your confessions, if you follow the dance of fashion in this world; and he who breaks faith with himself and with his creed, cannot hope for salvation that way. To be consistent, the believer in this view has no right to a minute's rest. Would you, had you been in New York the other day and heard the cries of the servant-girls in the fire, have felt that you had any right to be lying back in your fine carriage and pass along unheeding those burning victims? Could you allow yourself to tarry a minute ere you should rush to the rescue? Would you not even imperil your own life? Would you be a man if you didn't do that? But are you any more of a man, when you stand up in solemn sincerity and subscribe your faith to a belief that the whole world, not only by night but by day, is on fire, and souls are rolling by the billows of the generation into endless burnings at last, and yet believing this, ride easily along in decorous unconcern? Do you call such believing and such doing consistency? I don't say *you* do. I am only interpreting this view of saving souls. We ought to be up and sounding the alarm, every one of us, if things are so. And I honor the consistency of those fanatics who are consistent enough to do it. And if, instead of doing it a week or two in a year, they would do it the whole year round, I would honor them fifty-two times as much as I do. If this theory is right, then the ages have been right, and the old monastics were right, the monks and the hermits were all right, in abjuring the world and extirpating one half of their nature for the sake of saving the other half. They proved their belief by their works, and turned their backs upon life, its beauties and its joys, for the sake of a life to come. This is the theory.

How now about the facts? Let us look at this church, or any church in the world. Do churchmembers act as if they so believed? Does anybody act as if he believed it? You say, no. But I say they *profess* to believe it, and what shall we conclude? It is in their doctrinal books. I have heard it in Milwaukee, as elsewhere. But believing the *doctrinal part* of it, do they take the *other part?* Do they turn away from the world? Do they abstain from its pleasures? Do they not build fine houses? Have they no anxiety for life — I mean the believers in this very theory? Are they not seen at the opera? Care they nothing about fashions, think you? I am speaking of the consistency and integrity of the matter; of the question whether we affirm or deny in our practice, what we assert in our professions and belief. Let us look further.

Every man, every woman we see in the church and out of church, is industrious, devoted to some business, some useful pursuit in life; interested in making money, in building houses, in having fine homes, in the latest fashions; loving music, loving pleasure, loving childhood and childhood's glee and joy, — one as well as another. Do you see any of these believers — these saved ones, rushing through the streets sounding the alarm that the world is on fire — going to hell? Are they given up entirely to self-denial? Does practice look as if theory were a matter really believed at heart?

The keen observer of human conduct and human motives listens to the exhortation of the professedly saved soul; exhorting him to flee from the wrath to come; while the speed of this very exhorter, perhaps, in the chase after this world, outstrips the coursers of Dives. The little child sits still and listens to the instructions of its teacher. The bedecked and bejeweled believer in this way of salvation, set off to the last touch of fashion, warns the little life to avoid the vanities and shows of this world. The child is not old enough yet to stumble over the inconsistency of belief and practice; but by and by, from the still nest of memory a sceptic will be hatched, who will have faith in no religion whatever. Sanctimony and cant come of necessity, as the fruit of such contradiction. They cannot be avoided.

But in all this, through and through, you will find good people to some extent. They who believe one way in religion and practice another, if they are not the best, are not the worst people in the world. *Some* of the best that ever lived have believed just this way; but their goodness did not come from their denying in their life what they confessed in their belief; their excellence rooted in their *consistency*. They lived out what they believed; and we had better, vastly better, all of us, have a true, pure, noble life, though we have mistaken theories, than theories ever so sound, and lives that contradict them.

The whole matter then as it stands, is fraught with very instructive considerations. First, if any belief be *essential* to salvation, there can be no salvation except by *carrying out* that belief. Secondly, if it be right in God's sight to live in this world, and prosecute the interests of the present life, then no belief can be right *inconsistent* with that. Thirdly, such belief and such practice never did and never will harmonize. No matter what faith one may hold, as long as he lives there is a setting under-current of reason and common sense that will make him a child of this world and its interests; he will obey the laws which God has ordained over his own being and over the universe, in spite of speculative theories of whatever kind. Men will always live as they do, only better; that is, they will always love the things of this world;

they always ought to; it is duty to enjoy them and give God thanks. Any profession inconsistent with that, needs itself to be modified. And it is the pressure of this inconsistency, among other things, that is breaking up outlived theories of religion, and that makes the commotion of thought, conflict and confusion of ideas, in the religious tides of the times.

Cut a man in two, and you can't make either half of him live. Religion cut in two, half theory and half practice, each contradicting the other, is death. That is precisely what St. James meant by faith without works.

The trouble comes in here. In the first place, from false ideas of God. God is no such being as is represented in the theory. In the second place, from false ideas of man. There is not a man who believes such vile things pertaining to himself in his own heart. False ideas with regard to Christ also, are to be taken into account. Christ never died for any such purpose as the theory claims. False ideas with regard to human life make a great deal of trouble. Life and religion must never be contradictory; they go together. Any man who breeds a divorce between his religion and life must be wrong. The trouble comes, too, from false ideas of salvation. Salvation consists of two things, the curing of sin and the perfecting of nature. Life and religion must never be put in opposition. What saves a soul, is the application of truth to human life and character in such a way as to create righteousness and true holiness. No matter about theoretic and speculative views. Men hold nameless diversities upon this matter; but the one question of a Christly character is the test question of the Christian religion. He who is best in his character, according to the New Testament standard, is the best saved man.

Never, therefore, try to work religion against reason or science; you work God against Himself if you do. Never attempt to work religion against law; you work the very ordinance of heaven against its own enactments. Never attempt to work religion against humanity; religion is humanity's friend, sent to gather it up, to heal its hurts, and ripen its rawness. Never attempt to handle religion contrary to life; make them go together; bring them into harmony. Never set Providence against religion; true religion is always in the channel of Providence, and her voice and her ministry are God's second. Never set religion against common sense — common sense which is practical sense; and the most practical sense and the most useful sense is always religious. A man's hope of salvation is worth just so much as the Gospel makes *him* worth in his character. Consistency is among the heavenly graces, of course; but professing one way and doing the other, does not illustrate that consistency.

The great truth is, he who lives right will be sure to die right, and be right for ever. "Whatsoever one planteth, that also shall he reap." Myriads before any theory or profession was thought of, rolled up to glory over the sea of time, because they forgot not God, and lived under Him according to the best light and knowledge of their day.

God meant to save the world from the beginning.

As soon as He began it, He began to save it. The plan for doing it was ordained from the foundation of the world. The lambhood of God was then. God has been saving the world all along. He has never forgotten it. The ages have been in this interest; all history is but a record, in its place and in its way, of the development of this scheme of salvation. God is saving the world now. Whatever builds the finest and noblest institutions, is a power co-working with other powers in this line of salvation. Whatever creates the highest civilization, is exactly in accordance with this problem. Whatever shall create virtue in the world, purity in the place of corruption, develop truth in the place of falsehood and darkness, works in the line of salvation. Whatever produces the truest manhood, is sure to be saving in the scriptural sense. Whatever awakens the deepest and grandest in our nature, and brings it to affiliation with the grandest in the Divine nature, is sure to set the soul on the way of salvation. Whatever shall so fertilize the root of our immortality here as to prompt its growth, looks to its fruitage in the life everlasting, or saves the soul.

If life, then—if the institutions of life, the churches, the faith of the world, would just grasp these great, comprehensive truths, they would all be doing God's work of saving the world. If any soul here so believes and lives, he is so far saved. The faith in Christ that makes the life Christ-like, is the faith in Him that saves; the faith in God that makes character God-like, is the faith that saves in God.

Thus I have presented the two schemes. I am under obligation to you to set forth this twofold view. Don't let me force upon your acceptance either. Judge for yourselves. Choose ye which ye will adopt. My own view was given last Sunday. I don't believe this view—and for the reasons given.

But remember that whatever theories we may hold, good, bad, or indifferent, a theory itself never makes a man better, never makes him worse, any further than he applies it and works it. Would you be saved, remember that he that feareth God and worketh righteousness, of whatever nation, clime, or time in the world, may be, *will* be saved. The life, the character, as they contain and illustrate the life and character of the great Teacher Himself, is that which saves the soul. Salvation is not in word, but in deed and in power. He is saved who is completed in the scale of his nature. The worth of the Gospel lies in what it can do in this august finishing.

XI.

HELP—A SUPPLEMENT, NOT A SUBSTITUTE.

My help cometh from the Lord. — Psalms cxxi. 2.

Likewise the Spirit also helpeth our infirmities. — Romans viii. 26.

HERE are two texts, one from the Old and the other from the New; not two because of any divorce or antagonism, but the twofold form of one and the same truth; the God of the Old Testament, the Lord unto whom we look for help, and the Christ of the New Testament, the Lord manifest in the world; the Father on the one hand and the Son on the other; the Divine Spirit and the human spirit, thus linking grandly and essentially the twain in one.

Let me consider first this word *infirmity*. "The Spirit helpeth our infirmities."

We are the subjects of infirmity in three senses: first, by nature — in our raw *immaturity*. That is one of the forms and significancies of infirmity with regard to which we need help.

Again, our infirmities mean our *weaknesses*, debility, a lack or lowering of the tone even of native vigor — sometimes called sickness, but weakness is a good name.

In the third place, our infirmities are signified in the great ideas of *wrong, wickedness, vice*. What is sin? Sin is what is bad, morally. Sometimes men associate the worth of Christianity only with this latter infirmity; I do not wonder, therefore, that they show no more vigor, thrift, or rightness.

Next, consider the word *help*. " His Spirit helpeth our infirmities."

Help — a common word; it means aid, assistance, power lent; it means a recruiting, a reinforcement, and so on. The idea is plain enough. But you will notice that the help means power and augmentation applied, not to the wrongness, not to the debility, making it *more so;* not to the weakness, increasing *it;* but to the *subject* thereof — a nice distinction. Yet upon that hair trembles the life and death of the matter. We don't want to help immaturity, making it more immature; we don't want to add significance to debility, making it more significantly feeble; we don't want to make the wrong more wrong by any reinforcement thereto. But the beleaguered *subject* of these wants help. You want it and I want it; not that wherein we are what we *should not* be — enough of that already. We want to be made more and more that wherein we *should* be, *ought* to be, *can* be.

Again, help means not only aid, re-empowering the subject thus beleaguered, but it is no *supersedence* of his power; no *replacing* of his agency by something else; no suspension of it, no supplanting of it, no substitution for it. Help is a *yoke-fellow;* help is a supplemental armor put on for your conflict. It is something not to unsay, and undo, and prevent, and supersede; but something to *concur* with; an aid enabling what is to achieve success; whereas, without this enabling supplement, what is would achieve failure. Help, then, means co-operation, that which renders something else efficient; it means correlation of power, two powers yoked together, working together; not that the helping power should knock the helped one in the head, but that it should make it more and more grandly itself and finally successful.

Now notice the *helper*. "The Spirit helpeth our infirmities"—the Divine Spirit. It is a good rendering—"Helpeth our infirmities." *He* is the helper, for it must be a person. What is the helper? God the Father of the old dispensation; God in Christ, the typical and essential Divinity and power of the new dispensation. God, a Spirit in our spirit, the centre and heart and source of all vitality—that is the nature of the help. Hence I took the two texts from the Old and the New.

Having, then, thus passed upon these distinctions, notice now the *fitness* of this help for that which is to be helped; the divine adaptation to the infirmity out of which the subject is to be helped, and from which he is to be helped forever.

This Helper is no *arbitrary, ill-suited* appointment by the high court of heaven; He is touched with a feeling of our infirmities; not far off; not unapproachable; not unfeasible, but like us, to begin with. Then, again, this Helper is compassed about even with our infirmities, arrayed in the vesture of such fitness; and so He stands commissioned and adapted to us.

15*

In the second place, this help is *divine.* What we want here is Divinity. Put the neck of your humanity in one end, and that of Divinity in the other of the yoke, and you are yoke-fellows; that is, co-workers, working out together salvation. The Divine power not killing, and supplanting, and superseding in every sense the human power, but giving more power to it; passing its enabling virtue into the infirmity of sin, of immaturity, of debility.

Some time, when we get courage, we will have a discourse upon the humanity of God; for we are his offspring, you remember. If the child is human, is not the parent? It will do to think of until we have the sermon. Therefore we see there is the heart of humanity in this mighty help, as well as Divinity; human perfectness which helps, in connection with the divine perfectness, to fructify us, empower us, and communicate the aid we need to make our simple human endeavor successful in the great salvation problem.

In the fourth place, this help is *mighty;* sufficiently mighty; all-mighty; able to do and to accomplish ultimately even to the utmost what is needful; exactly the *mate* of all our infirmity.

In the fifth place, it is *hearty.* This help coming to us, comes as the result of no mere policy, no mere matter of head calculation, even at the throne, though it comes from headquarters. Hearty — what does that mean? It means the exuberance of the nature and power from which it comes; a surplus declaration, so to speak, of original investment in power and love. You can't purchase it; it is not purchasable. You fling profanation and blasphemy upon it when you propose to weigh it in the balance of an equivalent. It is self-balanced; it is a gift — *hearty*, original, unqualified. The fitness, then, mates on to the immaturity, for it is the life and summer power of God ripening our rawness; it is the mightiness and inspiring force of God toning up our debility; it is the purity of God cleansing the ulcers and poison of sin in our nature. Thus for the distinctions.

Now just take this help and go to the problem of salvation. You are saved when these supplementing powers are so accepted by you that your own powers carry out the purposes for which they are made. You are saved when you are helped in this threefold respect; when you utilize the helper; when you are helped to be *better*, or become better through these aids; when you become *stronger* in your goodness; when you become *riper* in your combined strength and rectitude.

Now, observe, the world has been figuring, and figuring, and figuring, for centuries, to find out how it can avoid the trouble of being good itself, and yet have all the advantage of being good. It has been trying to construct and solve a problem whereby it shall stand in the comfortableness of a good estate, without the trouble of rising to that attainment *actually* and *personally*. And hence we find that the world is willing to believe, until the end, in the goodness of *somebody else*, if that may stand in the place of its own goodness. Instead of taking such borrowed goodness as a *helping power* to make personal goodness, it takes it as a substitute. The world is willing to believe in the working power of another, and that another should do the work, and do all the work, to the extent of superseding the necessity of any work on its own part. It takes the help as the substitute for its own endeavor. It has been willing to do that, and to interpret the Christian's idea of help in that sense; thus slipping its own head out of its end of the yoke, and anxious to believe that the force applied at the *other* end will be sufficient for both. Vain illusion! Ungrateful beneficiary! Is that the kind of help we want?

Let me tell you—what you already know—that we want help in this matter of salvation, in this matter of our religion, on exactly the same principle that we want help anywhere. What is education? Your boy is raw, unripe, undeveloped in mind; he has certain weaknesses; in a certain sense he is feeble; quite likely already badly educated, perverted. You send him to school. He wants help. What does he want help for? Does he want it in the sense that he is called upon simply to believe that the university *is* a university, and to believe it with all his might? Does he want help in the sense that that university shall be a working power to release him from working? Does he want the school as a competent authority to make out the diploma and hand it to him while he masters not a lesson? Is that the help he wants? An easy way indeed to make scholars. Such help can be bought; but was it ever known to educate? What do you want help for? You want it that it may take hold with your powers, and so enable you to lift the whole burden. You want it to empower you so to work with your own endeavors, that your mind at last shall be developed; the competence of your nature brought forth and disciplined; the raw immaturity of the immortal material of your being, ripened under the helping powers of the grand tuitional forces,— you want that, exactly that, in education. And the man is a fool, and everybody says he is a fool, and the cry goes forth: The fools are not all dead yet, when he proposes to buy scholarship, buy education by some sort of trick or substitution that releases him from the work and the ache at his end of the yoke.

The help we want from God in this matter of salvation, from the God from whom cometh all help, is just such as the plant wants in order that it may get up out of the earth and grow and be perfected. Have these beautiful flowers sprung up without any aid? Why, God lets down his summer of warmth to help them germinate. He thus aids their uplifting energies to come forth all developed; so they get ability and glory beyond Solomon. The raw immaturity in the seed-life comes to beauty and purity. Your soul wants just such help as that, and God has given His spiritual summers, the fire and force of his own spirit, quick and powerful, stirring the latent germ in your nature. But a flower has not choice; it is not a person; it *instinctively* co-operates. *You* must do it *voluntarily*. That makes the difference between you and the plant. But the law and the method are the same.

What sort of help do your lungs want, for example? The help of the air, evidently. Why? So that the lungs can rest and do nothing, and have a good time, letting the air do all the breathing? The heart wants help. What sort of help? It wants the help of the stomach and every organ and function. Why? That the heart may stop and rest? That is the philosophy that reigns extensively in this world. Ah, the heart is the yoke-fellow of the brain, and the brain of the stomach; and each function of every other. That makes the harmony; that is the divinity of the whole.

So with light. The eye, in order to have good vision, wants the help of light; and the compliment may be returned. The light wants the help of the eye. Neither alone can produce the result. The ear wants the help of sound. The delicate musical instrument wants the help of skill in the fingers, and the frenzied genius of the musical soul. It can't do anything without it. Neither can the players do anything without the instrument. The instrument does not want the help of the player that it may do nothing, that it may not have a key stirred. No; correlation, mutuality in the matter is the law. In the production of water, oxygen wants the help of hydrogen; if you want to produce air, nitrogen wants the help of oxygen. Can you get water or air with only one element? Does the value of one element consist in its being a substitution for the other? Or does it consist in its *enabling* the other to perfect its power and reach the result? If you want the energy of steam, you put fire and water together. Water wants the help of fire; fire wants the help of water; not that the water should put the fire out and do it alone; not that the fire should drink up the water and destroy it; but, yoked together, the car starts.

So God and man come together. Man needs the help of God, not that he may lie idle, but that his human impotence may be capable of doing what it could not do without that help.

Now, is it not just so everywhere? How is it in your business life? A young man says, "O, if I had a thousand dollars; if I had five hundred; if I had just a little to ease me on here over this hard place; only warmth and sympathy enough to germinate me, I could grow." Let him have it and he will start; and then, if he has business tact, he will succeed. But should he say, "O, that I had my thousands that I might do nothing, dress finely, take my rattan and go forth about the streets, depending upon that substituted help to do my work!" Why, he could not get a place in a counting-room in Milwaukee. You would not trust him to carry a parcel from your store to its destination.

How is it in charity? There are hosts of beggars in the world. How can you best help them? By stuffing them full, washing them, and clothing them, and making them look like gentlemen? If you act on that principle, your charities, being a help to their inactivity instead of a stimulation to help themselves, damage the poor. It is no charity; it is a premium on profligacy and vagrancy; it is trifling with Providence. But if you can help a needy man, a hopeless, homeless man, with a kind word or a dollar that shall *start his endeavors;* if you can put an energy into the other end of his yoke in any way, do it; but don't do it in a way that shall slip his neck out. Otherwise, if you give him a gill, he will ask for a pint; give him a pint, he will ask for a gallon; give him a gallon, he will want a pailfull; give him that, and if you don't give him a hogshead next time, he will burn your house. It is a premium upon beggarism and loaferism, not only in the physical world, but even in the mental and moral world, to make help a substitute for endeavor. This dandling of spiritual subjects and trotting them on the knee of sentimental pity; this shedding of artificial tears over them until they are drowned almost in superfluous sympathy, never saved a soul any more than it cleared the guilt out of a criminal. But if the soul can be aided to do what it was made to do; to make use of all its powers in a right way unto their unfolding, unto their strengthening, unto their purifying, making use of helps that are necessary for that—that is divine; and beautiful is the life that gives itself to such help. Beautiful, indeed, are those who are helped in that way. That is the way to do good; that is the way to help in business; that is the way to help in charity, in want; that is the way the *problem of salvation is solved.*

Go out among the looms of Nature's handiwork; take the web and unravel it. There is the long thread running from the beginning to the end, and there are the needles that ply. How the needles want the help of the thread, and the thread the help of the needles! not that the one may be silent and do nothing, and be thrown away and counted as naught; and not that the other may be superseded; but that they may supplement each other, and the concurrence and mutuality of the two fill up the grand fabric of beauty and use, whether in star, or in flower, or waving field of grain; whether in university hall, in the vast problems of statesmanship and civilization, or in your closets; in your outlook towards glory; in the navigation of that voyage that crosses the dark sea. It is a law — this law of help. Here is the great problem of salvation. Work it out, then, with fear and trembling.

Why don't we take those aphorisms in philosophy and warm them until they seed our souls, and bloom, making our whole life fragrant? Why don't we go to work, co-work with God? I make an impeachment of God if, somehow or other, I propose to go on a flinty path until my feet bleed, so as to please Him enough not to bleed me any more. God is no such hard master as that. Go to work; use the powers that are in you, and the earth, and the air, and all the heavens are full of helpers that will flock to you and breed victory in your very impotence. That is what Paul meant when he said he gloried in his infirmities. He gloried in the fact that he stood environed by such a state of things, that when he was weak then he might become mighty. We want help to make us successful. The helper and the helped stand in this true relation to each other; and when they co-work the problem is solved, and the solution is salvation.

Now, I beg you not to figure that old problem, how you may get rid of doing anything by getting somebody else to do it for you, and still be just as well off as if you did it yourself. That day is waning. And don't you know that hundreds and thousands and millions who trusted that problem, seeing they cannot work it, are floating all adrift, not knowing what to do? They are called sceptics, a great many of them; and infidels, a great many of them; and cold-hearted and bad-hearted. And then there are others who resort to stirring up superficial, artificial, fitful feeling, depending upon that. A better day is dawning. The day of negatives is passing away, and the day of positives is laying its strong hand upon men, in religion as in business; and, like God in all nature, men have got to work until they work out a character like the character of Him who is the great motto and model. They must come to the unfolding, and development, and maturity of their own powers, obedient to God, according to the great plan by which that is done. Then Providence is God's helper, a grand presence. Then they work in the midst of the scheme that is vital in itself. We are born into this grand supplementary aid, created into it, candidates for its benefits, only with wills and not impersonality like the flower. If you want the blessing of God, keep the law of the blessing; if you want to be saved, solve the problem of salvation. God helps those who help themselves.

Salvation in the soul with regard to heaven, is not different as to the principle of it, from salvation anywhere, any problem in nature, any problem in life. It means success, not failure; conformity to laws, and not a violation of laws; it is the reciprocity of the human and Divine power; two wills concurring, two hearts in the relation of reciprocity; it is such use of God's power as renders your own power successful. When you find yourself striving, then, in the great conflicts and toils of life, friend, have a comfortable standing on which you can say, " *Thou, Lord, art my helper.*" When your own spirit consciously yearns toward the grand ultimatum, toward the ripening of the grand possibilities in your nature stipulated for in its make and in these helpers, then be consciously able to say that *God's spirit helpeth the infirmity of my spirit, ripening it, strengthening it, purifying it.*

On this cold, snowy morning, a basket of bright, blooming flowers came to my door; and as they passed up into the chamber of frailty and weariness, they lit up the cheerfulness of angel visitants. God, in all the storm and winter of our life, is sending down warmth, seeding this icy soil of our nature with bloom immortal. He is not a hard master; He is a husbandman whose garden is man's soul. He wants us to bloom in more than vernal beauty. He wants us to sing and breathe and be charmed in sweetness by and by, that shall make angel ministries to be forgotten and death the remembered mother of life.

As Nature, then, in her mute, unconscious order, reciprocates the love and help of God, so may you, O soul, subject of the living, conscious spirit, reciprocate the advances of help divine, bloom for bloom, life for life, glory for glory. Only reciprocate God in a use that shall not be abuse; then the heaven that you shall realize by and by, will be the ripeness of your nature, the glory of its strength, and the charm and sweetness of its unsullied purity — communicated by Him who bows down to man, that man in his earthly wants may be lifted to the fullness of the Father's estate.

XII.

MAN'S NATURE DEVELOPED BY THE QUICKENING POWER OF GOD'S NATURE.

My soul cleaveth unto the dust. Quicken thou me according to thy Word.

THAT is an outburst from the soul of David in one of his fortunate moods. "*The first man Adam was made a living soul; the last Adam was made a quickening spirit.*" So argues Paul, the apostle, on the great theme of the Resurrection. The Master said, "*Without me ye can do nothing.*" And He spake for universal truth and universal humanity. "*But I will make her desolate places like the garden of the Lord*," sighed out the old prophet from his soul.

These passages throw around my thought an atmosphere congenial to my subject; and therefore I quote them, as God quotes the summer on the sleeping germ in the earth.

Under the lead and spirit of these Scriptures, let me state and handle my theme for the morning, namely: "*The development of our nature as a spiritual organism, under the power of a higher nature as a spiritual organism suited to perfect and save it, is the true idea of religion.*"

Of course it is implied that this higher nature is fit and adequate, in all specific details and respects, to the work that is to be done; or, in other words, that the relation between the two natures is perfect and complete. This being the heart of my subject, I will not dwell upon minute details as to the fitness of this relation.

The great battle of all religious thought to-day, is prepared and is going on in the realm of human nature itself. All the searchings, all the inquiries, all the propositions, point to, and naturally are balanced and entertained in, this field and this precinct of humanity.

Come, then, to your own nature to-day. We find it to be in itself a living organism, to begin with; a sleeping embryo of everything that lies mutely prophesied in its structure and capacity. That is to say, man's nature in and of itself, was made by God a seed-plat full of germs, full of rudiments, full of embryonic possibilities and futurities. Our nature is rich in this human end of the problem of religion, enriched by what God deposited in it when He made it. I said, it was at first and is a vital organism, a thing of life and functions and organs; a germ of possible unfoldings, developments, growth, maturities. I repeat, by nature this is so; for all this I am speaking of, is man's human nature. Of course we mean faculties, powers, capacities, susceptibilities; hopes unborn, faith unawakened; all the constituents that enter into this wonderful organism of life and future possibility.

The next thing to be thought of is the great truth that those germs, seeds, or rudiments, however you may name them, need to be quickened by a life not in or of themselves. Their nature needs to feel the vital touch of some other nature; which last is to communicate its power and its quickening force to the first, in order that it may fulfill, and actually finish, and entirely complete, the plan of its being, and reach the end preordained for it, as well as in it, when God made it. These germinal potencies, these sleeping functions or spiritual organs, need to be warmed by the heat of a sun not in themselves, but far above them. They need to be breathed upon and breathed into; in other words, inspired, that they start on their career. They need to be cultivated, trained, tended, nursed and carefully handled. They need to be grown; they need to be matured. You will please keep in mind that this work proceeds under the power of a nature higher than the nature held under culture and tuition.

O, the wonder of this relation of man to God! The wonders and unspeakable marvels veiled in these hidden relations, circulating, I may say, in the blood of these consanguinities. O, the wonder of soul touching soul; of nature giving itself to nature; of life propagating itself in life! And yet why should we marvel, after all, at this great simplicity, wonderful as it is? For it is the most simple thing in the world. For thousands of years, and, for aught I know, we may say millions of years, God has been teaching this simple thought to the world. Every time He has commanded a warm sunbeam to penetrate a sleeping seed in the earth and wake it up, that lesson has been taught. Every time He has commissioned a new spring or summer to come forth out of its hiding-place, and breathe a new life into the torpid earth, He has taught the same thing — the lower nature quickened by the higher nature; a torpid, slumbering, undeveloped organism, pierced with the life and fructified by a high and sufficient organism above it — a counter-completing nature. These lessons and these rehearsals have been running on for ages, and for cycles unspeakable, inconceivable.

Precisely what God has taught in nature, we are to apply to spirit. This problem of our being in this grand work of religion and life, you perceive, is exactly in the nature of a birth. And I don't wonder at the rationalism of the New Testament that calls it the new birth. The soul born out of its ante-natal stillness and impotence, into power; the soul waked up to behold the world and order of existence it was actually created into; faculties unsealed, a sub-conscious life and world throbbing up into consciousness — born up, such is the idea. Beautiful figure! Literally true. It is of the nature of regeneration exactly. Marvel not at that dictum in the Book, when your very pathway is thronged with the affirmation of it in nature! The competency of this higher vital organism smiting the lower, rends the bands and bursts the slumbering, waiting, anticipating life there. It is exactly in the nature of salvation as well. Nay, it is salvation itself. To be saved is to be quickened by this power of life from heaven, working newness, working birth, working uplifting and completion in the first Adam or humanity.

Salvation, what is it? Is it a kind of battle-cry in your theologic warfare? Is it a kind of ceremonial function in place of altars made with hands? A routine or ritual adapted to the external temple and workings of sense? Salvation! A soul saved! What is it for a soul to be saved but exactly this, viz.: the rudimental elements of its nature inspired, vitalized, cultivated and cared for unto the end, even to a crown of ripeness and fullness and glory in another world?

And what is it to be lost, but just to be neglected? your nature left in its sterility, uncultivated, unquickened, unborn again? No rising from its grave, unregenerated; with no higher life piercing it, enriching it, strengthening it, or perfecting it: To be lost is that. To be left to rot in the native hill, wasting, perishing, is terrible indeed; but simple and plain as light; such it is to be lost. We lose ourselves.

Look into the depths of this nature! Look down into the dark deep of the soul, down to the deep-sea soundings! Descend to the latent life there, the sub-conscious world that you have never heard from, into which no vision of yourself has flashed; go there. Glory sleeps infolded, and bloom and wonder. Palaces there are waiting to be entered. Terrible blasts, howling and darkness and desolation are there, the nemesis of folly, neglect and falseness. Go down into the world within you, O soul! the world of human nature, and find what lies buried; exhume it and make a right use of it. That is the problem of religion.

At first, man is only slightly developed. A child, he awakes to feel himself touched by the aspects of the world around him. That is the primal, natural development. His intelligence becomes adjusted to the life he is living here in time and nature. He is busy to obtain a morsel of bread. This is his first rudimental development. But ere long, after that beginning, there is deeper awakening. Profounder slumbers are stirred, and there come cries for something which the morsel of bread will not satisfy. Whispers are born that say, "Man shall not live by bread alone." Other wants are revealed. Man wants what transcends the whole realm of sense and nature and matter. He wants spirit. Aye, better said than this; man wants the life, the love, the sympathy of another soul. He wants the fellowship of a mighty nature; the feeding of a Being mightier than himself, whose sympathetic bounty shall rain down richness into human want and human wasting. This is spiritual development. Man is now under the tuition of God, through providence and revelation and inspiration. And then, at last, there is a final development of man, a birth through the dark fiery gate of death. His very nature gets so awakened and so emergent in its conscious necessities, that the very bandages of time, the mortal wrappings of humanity, the old capsules, break and the prisoner flies away. There is a life beyond, then, waiting the issues of life here. That in itself is a high vital organism to work upon us. As it acts, the quickened nature within ascends, swelling and expanding all the time, heart meeting heart, being meeting being. A divine organism above, ever more mightily pouring life down into the lagging slumbers of him who needs it on the mortal path to the immortal.

This life beyond the veil is very soon hinted to us. I think of the present existence as parted off from that to come by a thin wall very much like a veil, almost transparent, and so delicate that the very pulse-throb of the great Nature up there, vibrates the medium and we feel it here. Sometimes we seem to see behind the veil faces of beauty unutterable, and glory looking through from beyond; and we just catch glimpses of them through the thin transparency. Then the vision once so caught, when it retreats, haunts us and haunts us evermore. We know then that the grand destiny and emergent tendency of soul and immortality in us, look beyond this visible to the great invisible world; and that the finished state of our existence is there. Oh, patience now, and gentleness and still life come down and talk with us, and sit by our side. Wisdom breeds her counsels in our thoughtfulness, tenderness in our hearts, and we are new. We are advised of the abiding interests our life elicits there, and we have no abiding city here.

Sometimes men think and speak as if they thought God were afar off; as if the spiritual world were far away beyond some grand stormy sea, above the heavens, at the end of a dark, returnless journey which we must all make to get there. But is it so? Is that other nature remote in distance? that other heart far away? That other world, does it lie in some mighty offing? and are we interspaced by planets and reaches and expansions of desolation? Is it not rather true that the whole of that mighty life-power already touches us, in our hearts if haply we may find it, warm on our lips, a divineness in our nature?

In this life — the better part of us, I mean, and that's all I am talking about this morning — we are in a slumber. Did you ever see a child sleeping on the grass, wearied by his summer play? Of what is he dreaming? He is among singing brooks, whispering leaves, singing birds, green hills, beautiful heavens, balmy airs, a paradise of sense. But it is only a dream. Let him actually wake up, and the world will no longer be dream, but reality all about him. He did not know it then. That dream was a prophet; the dream was an actuality prefigured. So this life is a dream. The invisible world is haunting us. Sometimes we feel the facile hand that preconformed our nature to it. And if we would only wake up, if we could be quickened by the higher nature as to the sleeping senses within us, we should not only see dreamlands, and singing brooks, and green hills, but we should see just what made the hills, and we could read the music of the very score on which the song was written. Sense in all its brilliance and glory would melt and vanish away, and there would be presented a new world. Even now God is here, and the spiritual world is here, and heaven is here to-day. All that grand conception of things invisible of which we speak so freely and so carelessly even — all is right here.

Sometimes men say, when their friends pass on, Ah! gone, gone, never to return! The golden bowl broken! the silver cord sundered! life's schemes mercilessly brought to wreck and disaster! But is this wisdom? One nature touching another nature, one life breeding itself in another life, one world down here infiguring itself in the soul, but to be exfigured there — is this the end and finish of life? Never. Death is birth. We pass on to promotion. There is only a resurrection in the transit, only new birth, the quickening powers of that higher nature of God vitalizing the higher powers of our nature. Life never ends. Life's work is never done. The grand organic life of God and the world of the translated, seizing the life of our nature, by its gales of inspiration sets the soul to rolling up its tides of unbroken being to roll on for ever. Don't the angels get heart? Are they not greatened every time one awakens and turns from the error of his ways? And may we not say truly that the infinite Soul comes to satisfaction reaped in no other way than from the travail that brings us onward, through all the stresses of the ascension, to the rest and finish that remaineth?

Angels help on the great Divine purposes to-day. Thousands of rays reflected from the burning throne, send down their summer warmth into the sleeping germs of immortality, quickening them to growth; countless messages flash from the world of translated and victorious life, athwart the dreary and waiting waste of our nature here, starting hope and faith from their slumbers, and setting them towards the city of God. The great world of organized life there, is potent upon the human world here to move it. Life comes down and plants itself in all its dearness in the heart-life here; and thus humanity lives anew and rises and enters into the great confirmations.

Deeper and deeper, then, go down into your own nature; for only as you do that, will you go deeper into God's nature. Down at the very bottom of your own humanity, sleeps the image of the Father. What you want to-day, is to awaken and brighten and develop it. Do you not know that there is no way of knowing God except through knowing yourself? A mere smattering or superficial acquaintance with one's own deep soul, is a mere smattering of God-knowledge and of salvation. In the human depths are the germs of immortality that need quickening. Buried there are beauties and wondrous nobilities just budding out, that need the summer warmth to encourage and mature them. Sometimes, indeed, they seem to be crushed by the rude feet of carelessness, and to perish in their birth. But the great truth stands, that no human blossom ever turned itself to God, that did not thrill the life — communication caught from Him — down to the very roots of faith and power. There is a great deal of perishing, a great deal of decaying, even when these germs are actually quickened into life and beauty. The old is left to perish, even as it is in the order of nature.

The greater part of the corn of wheat decays, to help the germ into life and growth. The one will decrease, the other will increase. In the depths of your nature you must search for all beauty, all grace, all manhood, all womanhood. Sweetness is born there, and the charm of blessedness. Nothing lofty is built of other material.

O, the depths in us! How they need to be stirred! How they need to be quickened! Sometimes God has to smite and rend the tough integument of the super-incumbent matter, that light and warmth may be let down into man's torpor. How the rudiments in him need to be quickened! How they need to be born again! How they lose who live a surface life — much in thought, more in heart — unspeakably in spiritual power! How unsaved we are; how un-awakened! No man can afford to live a day or even an hour in this world, unconsciously buried beneath the sod of his nativity. No man can afford to die thus, unawakened to a sense of higher things.

Here, briefly, is the problem of our whole being — the problem of our nature. Right here is our life-work. Exactly here is the matter of our religion, and here will read the record of our success or our failure. Draw aside the veil and anticipate the reading! The bells will ring out the proclamation as the verdict issues. Will they ring jubilees, triumphs, striking the great concords of memory and hope? or will they chime dirges, and requiems, and laments? Memory will live; will its under-chant be hope?

Now is the reconciling time; now is the day of salvation.

May God from heaven be the Divine quickening upon our nature, and may the wisdom that is from above make us wise unto salvation. In that we save ourselves through trustworthy fidelity in this summer husbandry of our nature, lies the God-given passport to heaven.

XIII.

A SUFFERING CHRIST IN NORMAL ACCORD WITH NATURE AND REASON.

A man of sorrows and acquainted with grief. — Isaiah liii. 3.

THESE words are supposed by many to point, prophetically, directly to Jesus Christ. The whole chapter is regarded as a grand vista through which faith beholds Him.

Many others look upon the passage as an outburst of Jewish aspiration, a gush of mingled memory and hope, bursting out of their sorrow and sighing, together with a passionate hungering for deliverance and the coming of God and their national fortune.

Do you ask me to sit as umpire between these two opinions? I must decline. I do not know so much about these things as many pretend to know. But if you will go into the New Testament, you will find all through that book, from the teachings of the evangelists, from the teachings of Christ Himself and the apostles, the great truth that He *was* a man of sorrows and acquainted with grief.

There is no mistaking this. We do not like to hear about this matter of sorrow always; and it is well that we do not. We are prone to brush up and burnish the old rusty spots, and with our wands sweep the heavens, until we see nothing but brightness, and conclude that shadows are a mere phantom, a defect of our own vision most likely, having no foundation in reality. But the stubborn *fact* is, suffering, grief and sorrow are not shadows of things, but things themselves. It is true, also, that they are set down in the Divine order of wisdom, love and power, written by a light in which there is no darkness at all. The simple truth is, this world of ours can no more do without heart-ache, than it can do without heart-ecstasy. And a man can never be a man without sorrow and suffering, any more than he can be a complete man without emancipation from sorrow and suffering. Why, the very heart of God is obliged to wade through conscious distress, that it may come, bright and dripping from the passage, into conscious deliverance and fruition of joy. There is a satisfaction to the Divine soul that comes only through its travail. But we must leave the general statement.

I have three propositions to enunciate just here:

First: If Jesus Christ stood the representative of God and humanity that he claimed to be, and *all the streams of history* poured their turbulent contents into his bosom; and if he stood also as a fountain from which throbbed the mingled streams of *prophetic life* — victory as well as suffering — then it is the most *natural* thing in the world that He should have been a man of sorrows and acquainted with grief.

We need not worry ourselves to link this fact to some miraculous, supernatural voucher or vouching. It is the most *rational* thing in the world, if Christ was what He claimed to be, that He should have been a man of sorrow and acquainted with grief; for what is all history but a fight, ending in victory or defeat? What is all history but a strife parturient, a grand life imprisoned and unborn, seeking deliverance and a crown? Nothing but that. And the jar and the terrible perturbations of humanity in all the pre-Christ ages, deposited their gathered tremors in Him, if his claims were true. And if they were true, the same economy of providence sweeps over the future that covers the past, and the central Fountain stands throbbing out this mingled power of joy and sorrow, the elements of conflict and the vouchers of victory, all through the unveiled centuries to come. It is the most natural thing in the world that a being who really was and is what Christ claimed to be, should be one of sorrow and acquainted with grief. That is the first proposition.

The next is: If Christ, with all his claims, be in this world no impostor, but a true, genuine being, having come for the sake of *working upon man*, and making mankind different and better, and not for the sake of working *upon God*, and effecting some *enabling status* in the Divine Governor and government of the universe, then it is the most natural thing in the world that He should have been, and should be, a man of sorrows and acquainted with grief.

Assuming him to have come for the benefit of humanity, and not for the benefit of Divinity; to have come bringing the power of God to make you different from what you are, and not for the expending of his own power to make God different from what He was or is. it is the most natural thing in the world — the most natural thing conceivable — that He should have been a man of sorrow and acquainted with grief. For, according to his own showing and according to God's showing, it was for simply this that He came, to bring the heart-ache of God into the world for the world's good. Jesus Christ is the divine importation of that spell and stress of paternal interest, which is the very life-power, when you feel it, of salvation in the soul. He came on a suffering errand; He came on a sorrowing embassy; He came to make you and me sorrowful after the fashion of the Father's sorrow. He came for that; and, putting it all inclusively, He of course came for nothing else. And when the element of divine sorrow over human dereliction, and divine yearning over human imperfection, becomes an ingredient and fact of character in your experience and mine, then the Divine heart has seen of the travail of its soul, and *is* satisfied.

Now, then, we ought by the reason to know, at this age of the world, that there is no such thing as handling the moral problem through whose solution man's nature is wrought upward, without suffering. You never can come into any good short of the cost of it. There can be no such thing as a resurrection that is not written and enacted in the very elements of death and victory over death. There can be no such thing as new birth, or higher birth, whose certitude is not vouched for in the pangs that produce it. Here is the secret of that high necessity. When sorrow is past, then joy becomes multiplied. So it stands a matter of simple necessity, a matter of simple rationality, that one who would bring God into an imperfect world and lift an imperfect world Godward, must be a power that has heart in it, and a heart that is capable of aching. Such the secret that is hidden, the distinctive essence in the root of the Gospel. So much for the second proposition — for I must be brief.

My third proposition is: That if Christ, being what He claimed to be, stood as the *vital link between two worlds*, a connecting artery between the life that now is and the life that is to come, it is the most natural thing conceivable that He should have been a being of sorrow and acquainted with grief.

For you know the way that we get out of one into the other, is through terrible aching. The way we pass out of life into life, from the lower to the upward, is by the dark gateway, through withering flowers, through vanishing melodies, through the way of scentless bowers, of fading beauties, of dying cadences, and all the mortal ecstasies that traverse our nature here. And what is this but dying? Dying — getting out of a world of death! What is dying but being born? And what is being born, immortally, but just *verifying* the vital connection between the two worlds? He, then, who assumes to stand as that fact and that power, needs indeed to be fraught with the whole significance of it. He needs to have occulted himself beneath the darkness of death; he needs to have come from the rending tomb of our nature, to have been buried in our nature and to have generated resurrection there. I am simply saying this great truth implies sorrow, suffering, tears.

Look out upon May. The harshest winds in all the year are spring winds. They put their raw, ungentle hands upon the harps within us, and these harps are chilled to silence; they sing no more. They issue their rough decrees, and life seems to wilt and wither; while all the time their meaning is, to nurture such frail things as fill this vase unto courage to bloom. Spring, the grandest season of all the year; spring, the very advent of God in sky and earth, always in sorrow and affliction stands by the bedside at Nature's birth.

Just so in religion. It always was so, and always will be so; hence no strange thing. It is a natural thing. We need not be troubled about arguing for or against supernaturalism or miracles. I never spent thirty minutes in that sort of intellectual amusement. A barren exercise this of pecking at the supernatural. Men may pile up as many folios as they please through the ages, and I will not pick a flaw in one of them. Still, the great truth against which they assume to argue shall live on, and throb on, and throb for ever; for it is founded originally *in the nature of things*. And the nature of things, or whatever rests in the nature of things, is *reasonable*. Whatever is founded in the nature of things, is among the most inevitable things in the world. Therefore, I say, for these reasons and others that I might add, it is the most natural thing in the world that the Christ of God should be a man of sorrow and acquainted with grief.

Ah! says one, so much grief, so much sorrow in a religion of joy! I thought when I got into the gospel, or the gospel into me, I had got done aching; no more anguish, nothing more of pain. I thought Christ came into the world to ache for me, whispers a sensitive demurrer. That is the old whisper. Ache for me that I need not ache at all; and my praises are due to Him that He did n't quail and that I got rid of all trouble, He taking it as my substitute. Yes, that is the idea of great multitudes. Whereas, the true idea of Christly suffering is the idea of a *life persistence*, as held for the time being in the thrall of imprisonment and restraint, and in the battle of death. The idea of suffering is the idea of *persistence of life*, greater than any contradiction that can meet or assail it; an idea that there is something in life superior to anything that can antagonize life, and that it will come at last to self-assertion and self-crowning. Take a homely illustration. A boy of twelve or thirteen aches from mere growth, as the persistence of his physical life fights the battle out of raw immaturity into the victory of manly strength. Ever is it the consciousness of having done wrong, that makes one ache out of wrong into right. The capacity for normal sorrow as normal life, treads the ascending pathway; the capacity for abnormal sorrow as it forsakes the ascending and turns to the downward grade, is repentance. Here lies the idea of the sorrow element in the economy of the world.

These are the truths we ought to celebrate to-day. We shrink and grow less and less every time we keep the sacrament as if it were the celebration of a suffering Christ who suffered in our place that we might live without suffering. It is when you fill up "what remains" of the sufferings of Christ, it is when you repeat them for the very ends for which they were taken and endured by Him, that the promise is yours. These great world truths should ring from us to-day. We should take these simply as a flag, and float it heaven-high, emblazoned with the mottoes, Love, Sorrow, Victory. It should blaze with these powers and inspirations. This is what we should unfurl it for to-day.

The communion season, at least for 1500 years of Christendom, has been regarded as a fence separating one class of people from another; the great divisive or partition wall to keep men apart; the assumption being, that those on one side are better and more like God than those on the other. They ought to be, certainly; if there is any justice in the separation they must be. But to be like God is to be very different from most of us. To be like God is to be possessors of grand inspirations, and grand principles, and powers, and virtues, and truths. It is to be the possessors of noble characters. It is to be the holders of grand personal forces, able to propagate themselves in the world far· and wide, furthering its redemption.

This communion service, rightly viewed, is not meant to divide but to bring the world together.

It does not care a straw what human church you belong to. It does not care a withered leaf what creed commands your name. It cares not an iota for human speculations. This symbol should be taken and lifted aloft by every soul belonging to the spiritual church of God. I don't say it is impossible for you to belong to the spiritual church of God unless you are a member of my church, or my neighbor's church, or some other church. Externally you may belong to no church. You must take all that responsibility yourself. The question is whether you belong to God's church, which is somewhat larger than yours or mine; whether you have taken these great powers and inspirations of conflict and victory, of character-making and Christ-making, into your humanity; whether they throb in your bosom, and are enthroned in regency in your life. If they are, then all other questions are secondary, and you belong to God's church. Very careful, therefore, should he be, whether Papal or Protestant usurper, who puts an exscinding hand upon you, if you belong to God's church.

I think this communion season should bring churches together, so far as they are worth anything. Churches may excommunicate each other, declaring no church is God's church but mine; but the moment we do that we cease to be Christians, and become pharisees and bigots. We drop Christianity and take up schism. We may say this man or that man is a Judas. But that don't make him so — nor unmake him if he is. Man is not commissioned for such work. Somebody else had better cast that stone. Judases never stay long at the communion. The atmosphere is uncongenial; they always go out and hang themselves. Nothing is to be feared from open, broad communion of all churches. God's way is to leave men free; to pour down light and life upon them, and leave the rest to their responsibility.

This great matter of religion is working down underneath and out of sight. A great many of you I meet from day to day, who are called outsiders — on the other side of the fence. You don't come in here; you say we will not let you come. And there is some truth, I suppose, in what you say. You hold up this testimony that we have in print here, the Creed and the Manual. Well, you have more respect a great many times for what is printed here, than we have for what you think is printed here. If you would just take our meaning of it you would be wiser. If you are a real Christ man or Christ woman, you belong to the great church of God; and you have no right to take your portion and hide it in your bosom or under your bed. We have no right to live here in Milwaukee in a religious and gospel civilization, caring not an iota for India, or Persia, or anything else. I excuse myself a great deal, and I excuse you; for we have been taught greatly a religion of selfishness. And yet we must remember that any man in the church or outside the church, who will do right and tell the truth because he is afraid he will be punished if he does not, will bear watching. It is just so with religion, through and through.

A man who wants to be good, pivoting on the motive of reward and punishment, could not be trusted out of sight of heaven's police were that motive taken from him. We ought to know that goodness is goodness for goodness' sake. I should tell the truth, not because I shall smart if I don't. Falseness should be ashamed unto death inside, though there should be no lash in the universe outside. If I am false, there is a terrible acid and blister working its penal results. Man should be beautiful in himself. I don't want to be doomed for ever to gaze into the looking-glass where things are not beautiful. I want to round out into true proportion and symmetry of being. Just be manly and womanly, and take these grand inspirations of the gospel as the earth is taking the sunshine, then you will begin to bloom, and be pure and beautiful in soul.

Be actuated by such motives, and the church of God will break down the partition-walls and bring men together; and the crown of their *character*, of their rightness, of their worth in God's sight, shall be the badge of distinction and the bond of union. Then we can unite in the long pull and the strong pull of moral forces, and the world will come together.

O for an abrogation of mere technical Christians, Christians by courtesy, Christians by position, like ciphers at the right hand of significant integers! O for the coming of the meat and marrow of things, for so we shall be judged at last. This is not disintegrating, it is integrating truth, Christ and life; it is construction, the very breeding of God in the garden of our humanity.

Keep mellow; keep tender. You never like to see a hard man or a hard woman. No man is the worse for being woman-hearted; no woman is the worse for being strong in that strength which nerves the very heart of Deity. Keep mellow, keep tender in soul. If you study the Bible, do not study it under those theories that make you wiry, bony or dry. You may find a great deal of fault with it. There is a great deal in it that doubtless would not have been there had the Bible been written a hundred years ago. But don't go to it with the carping and flippancy that leaves you like a dead dissected bird, songless as an epitaph. Keep clear of all that. Keep the bud in your nature warm and juicy and open. Then the very *atmosphere* of the Bible will be full of life-giving moisture, and feed you with its great stimulation. The first you know you will be blooming, and the next you will be bearing fruit. Men sometimes go at the Bible as a woodpecker goes at trees, only to find the worms. You will only be worm-fed if you do so.

Don't peck at Christians either; they are poor feeding enough. It is not well to whet appetites on the evils of mankind. They make diseased blood. Turn to the great model, the church spiritual, the Jerusalem above, which is the mother of us all. Greaten your nature and your conceptions of what is noble and charitable and true. One of the great uses of sorrow in the world is to keep its heart tender and great. We all know that joy is not perfected until it is brewed over the fire of grief. Sorrow dies in its culmination; after that comes the bloom of ecstasy. The last conflict is victory. Be gentle and you will be mighty. The more deeply human, the more deeply divine and godly will you be.

Embosom these truths in your confidence; broaden your life and deepen aspiration from their great life and power. God is down here among the fading flowers and the dying embers of life, to retint vanishing hues and relume the brightness that fades into shadow. Sorrow and grief are among the heavenly mordants that prepare the soul for the fast colors of glory, and help God to paint His name in it in letters living, indelible, immortal.

XIV.

DOMINION OF SPIRIT OVER MATTER.

As he prayed, the fashion of his countenance was changed. — Luke ix. 29.

THERE is a truth here — in this simple language — of deep and wondrous beauty. It shines out like a star on the face of night, or the glowing sun from behind his cloud-screens. Fire from heaven had come down and been kindled in its alabaster vase. Another glory beams out through the thin transparency, timeward. Light permeates the wall from within the temple. The vail itself is set aflame.

Of course we recognize in the text the scene of the *Transfiguration*. Many theories and speculations have been indulged in, respecting the nature and design of this marvelous incident in the life of the Saviour, but into these we care not to enter. About such facts, fancy has ever been, and ever will be, busy. Standing upon the boundary line, where the natural and the supernatural touch, the reason and imagination of man find themselves in a twilight where the costumes of fiction are very apt to personate sober fact, and all visions to stand at fault in the clear light of day. Men have put a great many things into the Bible that never had an existence even outside of it; and have drawn a great many things out of it that were never in it. Much of what has been wrought into what is called the sacred literature of Christendom, will vanish when the sun shines by and by; and no small portion of what men are pleased to call established scientific theology, will drop into forgetfulness as the mind of the world rises towards the zenith of its illumination. We should always be careful about anchoring to the past; it is raw, crude, and prevents growth. To regard the merely accidental and provisional aspects of truth as truth itself, is to mistake the chips of the workman for the statue or temple he fashioned. We can often get the spirit and inspiration of a subject long before we get the form. This is always the order of life; it clothes itself in its own form. Life is, from necessity, form-giving; but form is never life-giving. Therefore if we take the form first we get nothing but death. This is the curse of art and the grave of genius. But nowhere is formalism so dead and damaging to the soul as in religion.

We may say, however, this much with confidence, that in this scene of the transfiguration we have God set forth in the midst of the human race; a theophany wherein everything appears really carried into effect, which human fancy, springing from the real longings of the human soul, has arrayed in mystic forms, and thrown as a beauteous garb around the histories of other nations. All mythology is but the stammering of a true longing of the soul; a religious necessity, seeking to incarnate itself in the spectral shades of mere natural twilight. Without revelation the world worships the "unknown God." In the Bible where God clearly declares Himself, in the incarnate Word, transfigured, crucified, resurgent, glorified, these longings are met — legitimately met. Here are the great answers to the questions born in man by nature. Every picture in the Bible means something; every event is heavy with significance which our life stands in need of. All the gorgeous symbolism there, couches a glory or a gloom counterstated in us. And while we may not take the image for the thing, or the letter for the spirit, still the potent significance therein we may receive, and take it as a life which shall reclothe itself, through our experience, in garments of life and crowns of life.

The truth underlying the text, and upon which I would fix attention at this time, is far enough removed from all speculative and obsolete considerations, lying directly within our practical life. It takes us into some of the loftiest ranges of the soul's capabilities, and is at the foundation of all genuine and best culture. I refer to the power which all high and commanding themes have, taking possession of the soul, to manifest themselves in the character, asserting the dominion of spirit over matter, subjecting body to soul.

And the intimate connection of soul and body is the first thing we have to observe. As he prayed, the fashion of his *countenance* was changed — changed to a glow, lighted up, kindled. This was from no outward illumination, a borrowed light reflected from the surface. The lamp was inside. A fire was burning behind the transparency. There was a glory-lit passion of soul, deeper than the face, shining out through the face, which consumed everything in its own lustre, subjecting even physical functions to its own uses. There was a law within mightier than the law without; the sceptre of spirit flashing in the realm of matter; an orb of glory shooting up its kindling rays over the hills of nature, and filling the mental atmosphere with dawn and daybreak eternal. It was the dominion of soul over body.

The next thing we notice is the *fitness* of the one to be a revelation of the other. The face is the language of the soul; looks translate consciousness. It was because his soul was on fire that the fashion of his countenance was changed. The intimate connection between body and spirit, that enabled the conscious artist within to flash out its kindling visions through clay, and paint the shifting sceneries of the soul in the countenance, was asserted on Mount Tabor.

This is what we may know and see and feel in every hour of our life. The face mirrors the thought; sentiment kindles in the eye; storm looms and lowers on the brow; fear trails its shadow there, and hope sits like a sunrise. The countenance translates the mystic meanings of the life within. The face is a telegraph full of messages from the spirit world. The lines and phases and variations of expression we wear, are but the changes of the fashions, the wardrobes, gorgeous or meagre, of the feelings and fancies and moods that play themselves off within us. They are the windows through which the passers-by outside look in and behold the changing acts and shifting scenes of the ever busy, hurrying drama, ever playing but never played, on the stage of the world within us.

How grand is this fact, especially in strong, stormy, emotional states. When the Jupiter of the soul gathers clouds about him, how grandly sits wrath enthroned, muttering from inward thunders. The countenance can look an earthquake when anger and indignation put fire and water together down in the nether deeps of man's nature. The face is a tempest when the soul is stung by outrage, meanness and wrong; it is a boiling sea, a volcano. To-day you meet your friend in tranquil mood; the fashion of his look is serene and gentle as the summer evening. Beauty fills his soul, and sweetness and joy. To-morrow there is a cloud on him. The air of his eye is murky and heavy; blackness is everywhere, thunders are behind it. His soul is charged with sulphurous energies. A tempest is brewing; there is a storm in his spirit, and all the imagery of look and expression and bearing tell you so, and seem to say, Beware! They are soul revelations of the mastery of spirit over body.

How instantly sudden news, if it break the spell of long suspense with the note of gladness, will wipe out the night shadows and flood the face with morning glories; just as, on the other hand, if no hope come and the note be a knell, how will the same countenance droop into the drapery of the grave, and beauty dwell there in eye nor lip nor tone.

The outward appearance from day to day and from year to year, as our life flows on in all its connected changes, is but a panorama of the soul, the instantaneous photography of its vicissitudes, a long continued mnemonic gallery of the varying lights and shades and plots and scenic processions, of the sleepless and endless life within us. What history, what biography, annals how grand, poems, pictures, monuments, emblems wreathed with hope, and veiled epitaphs, legends of the heart, and silence, would all this record make, which a man builds up through the years God gives him. Yes: we are painting on canvas that shall outlast the face; we are chiseling on tablets, and carving on pillars, that shall endure when marble and brass are turned to dust.

But it is due that we notice with special attention, in connection with the truth we are now considering, the power and function of *Prayer*. For it was as the Saviour prayed, the record runs, that this glory came upon him.

It is probably no infraction of the laws of charity, certainly not the intimation of any, to say that, in the true and full sense of the word, only a few ever pray. Prayer is born of the soul, as streams are of fountains, or as ecstasies and agonies are of the heart. They cry out, or sing, of the deep within us. A prayer can never come out of the soul until it is first in it. First the consciousness, then the word that utters it. You cannot begin with words first, unless they are borrowed words. But these will be only as the dead leaves and dried roses of last year's stems.

You cannot use a prayer twice, any more than you can make a flower bloom twice. Even the Lord's Prayer was for the spirit of it, showing the manner of *spirit* we should be of, not the manner of words; just as Paul said he was a minister of the New Testament, not of the letter but of the spirit. The letter is dead. When a soul comes to God directly and puts itself into vital connection with Him, without any intervention of priest, altar, sacrifice, or word, then the soul becomes charged with God and gives off its sparks in words. The fire of his nature warms it up, kindles it, and it begins to burn and bloom, and sing or sorrow; and these manifestations are its prayer. But you cannot begin with words and get the fire out of them into you. Words are nothing but ashes that are left after the live coal within is consumed, the result and not the means of prayer. We go to God not to say things, but to be kindled by Him; not to communicate information, but to get inspiration out of Him; not to induce Him to change his purposes, but to get his purposes into us; never to bind Him, or obligate Him, or obstruct or even help Him, but evermore to say, " Thy will be done."

If men would pray in the Christly way, they would come to Christly experience. The fashion of their life's countenance would be changed. They would come to transfigurations of soul and manhood, and glow with inward revelations. Words never transfigure man. Transfigurations come from thoughts, from feelings, from exaltations. They come from things spiritual, unseen, and eternal; from what has power to awaken the soul, to fire the heart, to kindle the intellect, to rouse the conscience, to warm the sentiments, stimulate devotion, and lift the whole being through a glow of mighty urgency, toward the Source of all life. Transfigurations that foreshadow ascensions, must come from the powers of the world beyond. Visions from the face of the All-beauteous unveiled must seize men, and a direct, conscious intercourse with God the Eternal be had, if they would be transformed and transfigured into the spirit of his own likeness, luminous with the prophecy of heaven.

This is no dream; it is simply prayer. There is such a thing as the mind's losing itself in the infinite Mind. The human heart may yield itself to the bosom of the infinite Life and Love, to be kept and cared for. Man's soul may just turn itself away from beholding vanities, and look towards its Maker, and enter into sympathetic intercourse with Him. And when it does, that will be faith and trust. Then it will be touched with the all-kindling ray and pulse of his being. And when this is done, the *soul* will *pray*. Prayer will be born of it. Man will be consciously lifted and filled, and God will shine down into him and through him. His soul will be changed in its spiritual look, and the radiance of the immortal countenance shall not be hid.

Thus prayer ceases to be a constraint of duty, and becomes an ecstasy of desire. It is no longer an exercise in sacred literature, but a soul-passion before God. It is a liberated impulse of heart, playing in its utmost freedom; the glad, emancipated soul of the child, breathing its note of plaint or joy into the ear of the listening Father. In a word, prayer is immortal hunger eating its own bread, and spiritual thirst drinking at the life-giving fountain whose refreshing brings ecstasy to the eye, and color to the face, and bloom to the lips of even the mortal aspect, clothing it with a visible and prophetic glory, whose consummations are beyond these clay shrines of earth.

The power of prayer as an *intellectual* stimulant is very great. It will not solve problems in geometry, or give the sluggard daily bread without work. But the very act of prayer, if it be true prayer, throws the mind into the highest intellectual state as well as the deepest emotional. If you put the battery of the infinite brain to yours, why should n't it wake? The best prayers are always the best thinkers. For an intellect all alive with the Divine, Infinite Mind, will, of course, be intensely wakeful, living and richly productive. Prayer, of course, cannot paint a picture; but the soul of genius fired and set all aflame by inspirations from above itself, will be in the best condition to do anything. Up in the high region of prayer, immortal life shines upon the thought summits, and they are warmed down to the very roots. Summer gales come sweeping over the tropical land of the mind, and hidden life blooms out of it. Eternity sings in the heart, and new-born joy blushes on all the face of life, and man is glorified when he prays.

This is the preparation which all true men seek when they have any great work to do. When Moses communed with God in the Mount, he came down shining in face. It made Paul another being, when, in the heavenly exaltation, things were revealed to him which he could not tell. And apostles and martyrs have felt, in the rapt moods of all days, this stimulating force upon their minds for their work. Reason boasts of its independence of prayer sometimes, but it is a vain boast. As well might the April earth boast of independence of the sun in heaven. Intellect withers and freezes without this replenishing life and fire from Above.

But nowhere more than in the *closet* does this truth we are discussing assert itself. Many a hidden sanctuary is a Tabor. The devout soul in the closet understands this. Could mortal eye look in, when the door is shut, while some sainted soul is far up on its light-seeking errands, glory would be signalled in the countenance of the worshiper, and daybreak of other worlds. In no hour is the true man so serene in face, so tranquil, balanced, exalted and strong, as when he comes from the hidings of the inner life where God has been sought in communion. It is grand for man to be alone on the mountains with God a little while in the morning, before plunging into the rush of the day. He who never knows solitude will never reach true greatness. Man must be alone sometimes, or die. In retreats of mental loneliness and heart isolation, our sensibilities flood up into the purest light, and catch the radiance that gilds the prospect of heaven.

But touching the *power* of prayer, it must be remarked that it is in the *stressful* hours of the soul, when it is in straits, when a world hangs upon it and it is pressed by some mighty urgency of impending woe, that prayer has its greatest power. God is most to us when most needed, in times of heartbreak, when we go down into the valley all alone, and the world is sunless. Then He seems to come and break over the barriers that wall Him off from our spirits, and leaps down into the heart of our intercessions, rolling away the mountains, lifting the clouds, and swallowing up all the old night of despair in the fresh brightness of his presence. Prayer then becomes a transfiguration that converts even death into a revelation. The vale of darkness becomes a Tabor, and the drapery of the grave an ascension robe. Thousands have emerged from their prisons singing, and gone up with radiant look in chariots of flame. Thus it was with Christ when he strengthened himself for his hour. His soul was in transfigurations while a world hung upon him. In that night of darkness God tented, and a glory was lit there from beyond all veils.

Somehow it seems to be ordered that no face shall shine sweetest till the shadows have passed over it. These prepare it for the higher burnishing. Sweetest tones are born of complaining discords. God and heaven come to us through the cross. The scenery of the natural heavens is never so grand as when hung with dark convolutions of cloud-drapery, when the sun is behind, shooting his radiance through the folds, and kindling it all into burning throneglories of sapphire and gold. So with the soul in the spiritual clouds. If God can come into it then, its sky is transfigured, it is a burning temple. And prayer is the torch that can kindle that flame.

But let us advance a little for a different view. The truth we are considering is not limited to the sphere of prayer, *technically* so designated. Whenever any great and glorious subject takes hold of the mind powerfully, it is of the nature of things that it should be lifted to higher planes of light and force. High intellectual pursuits report themselves in the bearing and manners of men. The general aspect of life is their revelation. The atmosphere about such lives is surcharged with latent meaning. As a general thing, men who think best look best, behave best, enjoy themselves best. A good soul makes a good countenance. A fine, intelligent spirit, with the fires of intellect burning inside, will light up plain features and make even homely ones comely. Cosmetics will not do this, but thought will, beautiful sentiment will. Fine and lofty feelings will glow there as gold in sunsets and purple in dawns. The vernal fires blazing within will keep bloom outside and keep off wrinkles better than the sorceries of the toilet, and send the violets blooming down beneath the snow-crust of years. I have often wondered that the beauty-loving passion of our race did not take more pains to plant the seeds of immortal youth where they would be most likely to live and give back their verdure and bloom perennially. The greatest thing God ever made of clay, is the human countenance. Sometimes it is nothing to look at of itself, cast in no model of symmetry, grace or majesty. Like porcelain transparence, such may present neither comeliness nor meaning of themselves. But let the fires be kindled on the other side, put the light behind the transparency, start the flame in the candlestick of the soul, and lo! all is transfigured in a moment. The clay becomes glorified. Beauty that is fadeless beams and trembles in every line, and glows in magic tracery on the veil.

The fine moods of genius are all fulfilments of this law. It flings its inspirations outward. Here the soul is artist, incarnating ideals. Milton's face was a thousand times a poem. Beethoven's symphony and Raphael's transfiguration the canvas never caught, while his of Patmos was a New Jerusalem come down out of heaven from God. The fashion of the countenance may be the grandest rehearsal of inward glories. It is every one's duty to keep such a fashion. Some inspiration should be shining out all the time. God made the countenance to be a reminder of Himself. It should speak or sing or glow from some spark struck from its Maker, that the night side of the veil may hold the promise of morning.

Even the ravages of time may be stayed to a good extent by the high dominion of spirit over body. It is not needful that souls grow old. Strong fire may burn upon wintry hearths, and the bud and bloom of immortal youth may be putting forth from the interior, while even the outward husk is dropping away. Time will make the veil only more transparent if we say so. The brightest glories may be mirrored at last.

Thus have we turned the phases of our many-sided theme. One thing stands foremost: *The soul is king;* the mind is the man. Whatever is uppermost in character is apt to be conspicuous in life and behavior, and will name us when life and all appearances are done. . What were these bodies, the finest look flashing with nameless wonder, were they not the spirit's shrine? What but a casket without a jewel, dark lanterns, lumps of clay, fireless shadows!

The face, then, means *character.* The general aspect and bearing, the air and expression which fix the individuality of the man, are determined by the thoughts that populate his brain, the feelings that animate his heart. This does not mean to contravene the general statement that appearances may deceive, but to affirm the truth that the general atmosphere of one's personality is determined by the character of his inner life. Strong purposes outline themselves in the features; strong passions burn and cut their deep channels where lines of beauty ought to curve. And how gross and grovelling propensities trail their muddy records where signals of glory ought to be flying; while care furrows and discontent wrinkles the brow of life, and vanity flutters her telltale signals in every breeze. Just as, on the other hand, calm sereneness on the summer sky, light on the distant hills, tell us how beautiful feelings repose in human looks. Sweetness and serenity of spirit lave the countenance with the hues of other worlds. All beauty dethroned within, makes the outward temple a ruin — a wreck and chaos. Beauty lit, and her lamp burning at the centre, throws out her luminous shadows all around, outlining a temple imperishable.

At any rate, there is a glory which man reaches *only* by the pathway of highest thoughts, those that are truest, noblest, most regal in themselves. Hence it is a sacred duty as it is a privilege abiding with every man, to live above himself, to keep the company and be under the draft of endeavors and aspirations self-transcending. This is the marvelous boon of being. Upon just this ascension path Christ came to put us and lead us. Such is our nature, that unless we rise we inevitably sink. God has made us expectant of new and perpetual morn. We glow in true lustre only as we near the purple gateways. If we turn the organ of spiritual vision downward to darkness, it perishes.

But just because our ascension path is a stairway of the highest, noblest thoughts, are we obliged to come at last to *religious* thoughts. There are no highest but these. No others take us on to a life above nature. These do. God is in them, and they are God in us. Here is immortality. All fire of soul that shall not go out, emanates from this sun. The fadeless flowers of mind and heart bloom from the quickening touch of this summer life. No soul can live without religion. It will shrink and wither, and become lean and haggard and lost, untransfigured.

And so here we come round again to the great fact we started with, viz.: the highest form of religion in conscious exercise is *prayer*. It was as he *prayed*, we remember, that the fashion of his countenance was changed. Here is not only the soul's hunger, but its feeding, its reception and assimilation of the divine nurture. We come to banquets in this uplifted consciousness, into the tinted glories of peace and life; we pluck rays from the eternal Mind; we take God into the soul when we pray. Here is the mount; here the truest transfiguration to us mortals here in time.

But more grand and glorious than any fashion of countenance, more expressive than any mirrored ecstasies of thought or sentiment in the human face, is that embodiment of truth and power which is contained in the sum total of a good man's life. What we signify of soul and being in the connected phases and changes that make up our moral probation, the finish of our manhood and womanhood, this is the great verdict of the question on trial. If *life* be divinely transfigured, then comes color to its earnest countenance, which the blood of cleansing meant to give. The soul beams forth in this great broad outlook, an earnest of the life to come.

And then, when we come to think of it, how do we know but these countenances of time shall be familiar in eternity? These old personalities, the illuminated looks and remembrances of to-day, immortalized? What shall we be there but just these?

Be it ours, then, to see that the lights are beauteous; that the fashion of the immortal countenance be like unto that of the Son of God. Heaven is the soul transfigured with celestial brightness. No look of sin or shame or sorrow shall be there, but the glory of the Lamb lighting it with eternal day.

There was once on earth a perfect life; it was cradled in innocence; its childhood was a summer day of veiled light and waxing wonders; its manhood stern, stormy, grand, but gentle; and its exit a convulsion that shattered the prisons of darkness and despair, and planted the signals of eternal disaster over sin, death, and hell. It lit the torch of hope on the pathway of mortals, and left it burning, and then passed into shadow. Be it ours to follow that life; in the dawn and in the noonday; down through the valley and up the ascension path; till, with Him and Elias and Moses, and all the glorified, we come to the great assembly at the right hand of God.

XV.

DEBT? — OR GIFT?

Hereby perceive we the love of God, because Christ laid down his life for us.
1 John iii. 16.
Greater love hath no man than this, that a man lay down his life for his friends.
John xv. 13.

PERHAPS some of you noticed, the other day, that President Finney, in conducting a communion service of several associated churches, I believe, invited not only members of all churches to remain, but in addition to church-members, invited also persons not members of any church, who, nevertheless, wished to be followers of the Truth and Life, to tarry at the service. That was Mr. Finney.

I endorse the act heartily; and I only wait for the time to come when all the churches shall endorse it — for the time surely will come. And if this church is ready for it, and by vote or any other way will commission me to give that invitation, I shall be ready. I am outgrowing artificial distinctions more and more every day. A man is a man, true or false, and a Christian is a Christian, not by virtue of the pew he occupies, the church he attends, or his ecclesiastical status, but by virtue of his character and essential worth before God.

If any of you take comfort in so thinking, I am

glad. But you must remember, also, that while you have comfort as a man and a Christian *outside*, there are a great many reasons why you should rejoice in all this *inside*. Christianity and manhood *organized*, make an institution of unspeakable power. A church, animated by a sense of its own proper significance, is a spiritual engine in the world for truth and virtue, whose potency is without a peer. It asserts God; scatters light; educates and exalts man; and is the new spiritual kingdom in its measure. Men come into churches under the laws of affinity. True men seek their affiliation not artificially but spiritually, sympathetically; not to be saved, but to *assert the power* of salvation. The force of each is thus multiplied by that of all. So we give the usual invitation this morning, subject to the judgment and conscience of each one.

And now I invite your attention to these grand words: "*Hereby perceive we the love of God, because Christ laid down his life for us.*" Here, at any rate, the death of Christ expressed the love of God. Again, in the gospel of John: "*Greater love hath no man than this, that a man lay down his life for his friends.*" Exactly what Christ did. But that is not all. Listen further: "*God hath commended his love toward us, in that while we were yet sinners, Christ died for us,*"— for foes even, as well as friends. Broader even than Mr. Finney, Christ is. And why all that? *For God so loved the world that He gave his only Son that whosoever believeth in Him should not perish, but have everlasting life.*

I know these are picked passages. The Bible is made from the Divine *head* and the Divine *heart*, and these passages come from the heart. They are representatives of the heart class generally. But somehow there is a general feeling of consent throughout Christendom, that the centre and saving significance of the gospel is *heart power* rather than head power. It is love rather than law — *life* as distinct from *light*. Indeed, John says the light is life shining. It is a matter of general agreement, moreover, without qualification, throughout Christendom, that Christ *died*. All who believe that He lived, believe that He died. There is no diversity of opinion on this. Again, it is an universal consent and testimony that Christ died *for us* — in some sense, that He died *for men*. Again, also, it is the universal belief, standing in general testimony, that in some sense Christ died to *express love*. As in the text, "*Hereby* perceive we the love of *God*, because Christ *laid down his life for us*." That is what he did it for, to express God's love. So that, generally, love is considered the central and essential substance of the gospel.

And yet we all know that the New Testament abounds in statements from which men have inferred that the death of Christ expressed not the *love* of God, but the *wrath* of God; passages from which they infer that the death of Christ meant God's penal anger; that it means *punishment;* that it means *penalty* — the high exactions of justice as distinct from the free gift of grace and love.

Now this view of Christianity is called, by way of

distinction, the "*satisfaction*" view. It is expressed thus: "*Divine justice receives satisfaction for the sins of men by the substituted penal sufferings of the Son of God.*" This is sometimes called also the *commercial* view of salvation, or of Christ's work, as distinguished from the spiritual and gracious view. Hence certain terms rife in the handling of this satisfaction or commercial view. For instance, the conception is that we owe a vast *debt* to God, and Christ comes and offers Himself as payment of the debt — the word *debt* being a commercial term.

Again, salvation, or the benefits of the Gospel are conceived to be a *purchase* from somebody — from some power possessing the desired boon; and Christ, in dying, becomes the *price* of that purchase. Thus, also, under the same view, we come upon the word *ransom*, which is in the Bible; the idea of which being a redemption back out of captivity, of one who has been captured by a hostile power. Christ paid the ransom — paid it by his agony. Other commercial terms come into use, as when men say, the suffering of Christ *liquidated* the claims of the law; Christ was *substituted* for our *indebtedness* — commercial terms. Again, he took upon himself our *liabilities*, and God imputed them to Him — words indicative of a commercial transaction. God accepted him as our *surety;* as if we stood in account with God, and being insolvent, utterly bankrupt, Christ steps in, bringing so much agony-money to pay the deficit on the balance-sheet, and thus square the account with God. Christ constitutes a grand credit entry in the profit and loss account, that makes us good with the Divine government. God is *satisfied.* Christ is his *legal* quit claim. These are the satisfaction and commercial views of salvation, as indicated by the terms selected for handling it.

Or, should the matter be contemplated under a simply *judicial* aspect, we find coming into use another set of terms indicating a criminal status of Christ, and the action of penal law. For instance, Christ is conceived of as a *victim* demanded by *outraged justice.* Christ is conceived of as a *bloody sacrifice* to *propitiate* God and win back his lost favor. God is thought of as *punishing* Christ for our sins; or, is viewed as putting the *stripes* that belonged *to us* on to *Christ.* Christ is conceived of as bearing the *penalty* of our transgression. And this is the way He satisfies the claims God holds against us. The laws and status of the Divine government in relation to man, become changed by Christ. Christ reconciles God; satisfies Him; enables Him thus to go forward in the work of salvation.

This, you know, is what is called the *Calvinistic* view of Christianity. Not that Calvin originated it three hundred years ago; not that these ideas were never in the minds of men before the days of the great Reformer; but that master-mind gathered up the elements of the grand system and codified them, being of legal bent and training himself. Having not only an acute, but vigorously logical mind, he compiled and compacted this iron system, called the satisfaction system, or the commercial system, or the legal system; so that it not only bears his name, but it has held the faith of mankind greatly from that time to this. I can give it to you in a word. Calvin, in his Institutes, says:

"Had Christ been murdered by robbers, his death would have been no satisfaction to God; but when he was regarded as a *criminal* it was incumbent on him to feel the severity of *divine revenge*, in order that he might both ward off and *satisfy* a righteous sentence; wherefore we wonder not that he is said to have descended into hell, since he endured that death which is inflicted by an *angry God* on the wicked."

This, you perceive, is exactly and logically the doctrine of *substituted* penalty, never so forcibly put as by this great intellect of Calvin. Our sensibilities start back, I know, in this day, from such views of God and his gospel; and nine out of ten would probably disown all faith in them. And yet, touch one stone in the arch and the structure comes down. Break one link in the chain and the rest is no better than a rope of sand.

If we take the standpoint of the Westminster divines, the severity of their views on the doctrine of God and Christ, is quite as vigorous as anything we find in the Genevan Master. They could say: "The Father chose the objects of mercy; the Son *purchased* redemption for them. By the decree of God for the manifestation of his own glory, some are predestined to everlasting life, and others preordained to everlasting death. God was pleased to pass them by, and ordain them to wrath for their sin, to the praise of his glorious justice."

Now, I do not cite these different systems for the sake of *criticising* them. I bring them forward to show the difference between the commercial view and the spiritual view; between the debt view and the grace view; between the law view and the love view; between the arithmetical view and the ethical view of the gospel. The difference comes upon our thought by such questions as: "Does God demand pay for our indebtedness as if He came forth as any other collector, taking us by the throat, as the parable has it, saying, pay me that thou owest? and does Christ step in and pay the debt and let us off?" or, "Does God come forth the forgiver of our debts, sending Christ into the heart to tell how it is done?" He cannot do both — *collect* the debt and *forgive* it too. Is Christ punished instead of ourselves? Or does Christ come into the world God's offer of pardon on our repentance and forsaking of sin? For he cannot *pardon* and *punish* too. No matter whether God deals with you or your substitute. If the debt is *paid*, or the sin *punished* in any way, pardon and forgiveness as *grace*, a *free gift*, is simply absurd. The only question is, *which* is the gospel, grace *or* debt? punishment *or* forgiveness? pardon as a *gratuity*, or pardon purchased and *paid* for?

The mighty matter turns on the interpretation of words, and the genuine conception of the work of Christ. Did Christ come to reconcile God to man, or man to God? Do we conceive his design to be to change the status of the Divine government towards man, or to change the status of man's character towards the Divine government? Does Christ by his life and death contribute any competence to the Divine government not originally inhering in it? or is he in the world to make known and to execute the unoriginated and eternal competence of that government?

Honest men have held both views; good men have held both, and they hold both to-day. There is, I add, truth in both schemes; for you cannot find a scheme of faith in history that has not had some power of truth in it; and it is the truth that holds men.

Doubtless there is a high point of view which the human mind and heart will reach by and by, from which this dual aspect of Christianity may be viewed, and seen to be in harmonious adjustment and oneness in itself. When we leave human theories; when we leave artificial schemes of thought; drop the syllogism of Aristotle and walk in the inspiration of John; then we shall begin to feel even within us the sympathetic affinity of truth in all its diversities and divorcements, and we shall walk not only in the grace of Justice but in the justice of Grace.

When men pass by the human media, discolored by time, by circumstances, by individuality, and come directly to the text itself—nay, rather, when the providence of God shall raise up a fresh generation of thinkers that never knew the constraining bias of rhetoric, art, conventionalism and speculation, coming directly to the fresh words of Christ, then we shall begin, or the world will begin, to grasp the oneness, and feel the vital force of the harmony and ingenerating and regenerating power of truth and life, — the eternal embrace of justice and love. Even now love is as exact as justice is gracious. There is not an attribute of God that may not be enunciated by the lip of any other attribute. There is no separate interest; there is a mighty harmony eternally there. Old Mercy herself is just, and Justice is merciful. And this breaking things asunder which God has joined together, is direful misfortune in the thinking and faith of the world. Law itself is gracious, and grace is equally lawful; righteousness and truth met eternally ago; pardon and penalty melt into *one* in the Father's heart.

Let us then, this morning at any rate, seek the higher point; let us endeavor to emancipate ourselves from the thrall of the lower love. Let us not linger among the conflicts and the jars of mere human thinking, but turn from human doubt to belief in God. Do it by your heart; do it by your spirit; do it by your faith, your whole soul. It is your right; it is your privilege, especially, to hold no view that shall chill the debt of *gratitude* in the soul, from the fact that your *obligations* seem to have been *cancelled* by another. Drop not religion down to the level of a mercenary transaction — to a mere commercial adjustment. Hold yourself an infinite debtor, but to love and forgiveness without price. Chime in with the old angel-song, "Glory to God in the highest, peace on earth, good will to men;" God so loved the world from eternity of his own motion and nature that He sent Christ to make known his love and apply it. He came even to the cross, to the grave, and out of the grave, to the manifestation of that love.

To-day, then, we stand on these *heart texts;* for the communion day is a heart-day. We perceive the love of God now, *in that* Christ laid down his life for us. "Greater love hath no man than this, that a man lay down his life for his friends." But more was done than this, in the fact that God commended his own love toward us, *in that* while we were not friends but sinners, Christ died for us. All coming out of the original germ, that God so loved the world that He gave his Son, that whosoever should believe in Him should not perish, but live evermore.

Here we are safe; here we can be grateful; here we melt into penitence; here we bloom in hope. We can take our stand now with ancient Paul himself, who said: "I am crucified with Christ; nevertheless I live; yet not I, but Christ liveth in me. And the life which I now live in the flesh, I live by the faith of the Son of God, who loveth me and gave Himself for me."

Let us stand there to-day, not chilled and shivering as culprits fearing sentence, but exultant and jubilant under the grand grace proclamation of life. The prison-doors are open, the culprit chains are shattered. The Father has spoken. He has bread for the hungry, and healing for the sick, and outstretched arms and insignia of honor for every returning prodigal.

XVI.

DRAWING NIGH UNTO GOD.

Draw nigh unto God and He will draw nigh unto you. — James iv. 8.

THIS is a movement, not of antecedence and consequence, but of simultaneousness. When two are together, one is as the other.

The text therefore enunciates a great principle in religion. The principle is: if you want a blessing from God, go to God for it; use the rational means therefor; fulfill the conditions of receiving it. If you want anything from the market, go to the market for it and it is yours. Do you wish education? go to education for the gift, and education is with you. Are you in frailty, seeking health, sighing for her rich fountains? approach them and her benedictions are yours. Are you an aspirant for honor? rise to honor and honor is yours. Do you hunger and thirst for purity? you have nothing to do but to be pure, and purity is with you — not otherwise. No matter how much faith you have in purity; no matter how abundant and inspired your hymns of praise to purity; if you desire her, be pure and she is yours. Draw nigh unto anything, and that to which you draw nigh, draws nigh to you; that which interspaces you vanishes, and the proximity ensues in the premises.

There is a great deal said about drawing nigh unto God; a great deal of talk about living near to God; so much that we are quite familiar with it. I often think we have lost the crisp, contractile force of the idea, allowing it to drop into mere cant.

Let us see then, if we can, what is really meant by drawing nigh unto God.

Not *spatially* is it to be done; for the distance between God and any soul is not a matter of space at all; it is not a matter of interstellar or planetary ranges. God is just as near to you on the Pacific as on the Atlantic coast; just as near on the further continent as here; just as near, notwithstanding leagues and leagues may interspace point and point, or being and being. Take the wings of the morning and dwell in the uttermost parts of the earth, and God is there as much as when and where you started. Make your bed in hell — He is there. The separation is not, in any sense, a matter of space or time.

Neither is it a matter of mere existence, or a *metaphysical* distance; for in Him perpetually we live and move and have our being. God touches all being at all times, and under all possible conditions. Therefore this is not the difference.

Neither is it that of *officiality*. God is no more remote from one soul than from another as to his Fatherhood. He is the Father of all men. He is the judge of all alike. He is the universal lawgiver. He is the governor over all; the bountiful provider for all. He sendeth rain upon the just and the unjust; and He is no respecter of persons. *This* is not the distance and the difference.

But this it is, viz.: *Distance and difference of character;* a disparity, not of being, but of *quality* of being.

I think you will sometimes be tired of hearing this word character so often in connection with religion. It is a pulpit innovation, perhaps; and yet it is all there is of religion. Eliminate this, or leave it out in any way, and the rest is a mere spasm or phantom of cant. The difference that needs to be overcome in your approaches to God, is the difference between his character and yours, and nothing else. We draw near to Him when we approximate his likeness in the quality of our virtue, of our nature — in a word, of our character.

But, ah! what is character? says some one; what is it? how is it made? of what does it consist?

We are told that we are created in the image of God; which means that we have certain capacities, certain powers, faculties, elemental constituencies of our nature, the immortal humanity deposited within us, by virtue of which we are capable of becoming like God. In this sense we bear his image. Image is prophetic; image is an outline possibility; a competency.

In this respect we have three main elements: our intelligent nature, our moral nature, our spiritual nature. Our intelligent nature relates us to God under capacities of receiving truth. It is the truth-acquiring possibility within us. Our moral nature enables us to be right instead of wrong, or wrong instead of right, as we determine. It enables us to be righteous. We are thus capable of repeating the virtue in God. Our spiritual nature or capacity is that by which we can be receptive of the Divine, and become subjects of the life and inspiration of God. God may glow in the torpor of our nature through an elemental relation to Him, deeper than thought, deeper than virtue, through that radical endowment of being whose root drinks life directly from Him.

Now the development of this threefold competence of our nature, the balancing of all the powers therein, the putting to right use of everything that makes us, is the function and the fact of character. No matter how your associations may bias you; no matter how like a sweet morsel you may roll something else under the tongue of your memory or hope; your religion is worth what you are worth in God's estimate as to your character; nothing more.

So that this drawing nigh to God, you perceive, is no artificial matter; it is no mechanical contrivance, no dead paint or formulated imitation; no pantomime or simulacrum whatever. It is a moral significance involving virtue, right, purity and all the excellences and graces of human character. It involves, as we have already seen, not only the moral element, but the spiritual element; the exercise of the deep, ultimate capacity in human nature for receiving God, and all that is sweet and divine and ecstatic within Him.

To draw near to God artificially, is very much like drawing near to these beautiful flowers by way of silk and satin and paint. It can be done; and the unpracticed eye shall be cheated We can imitate, but it will not be the thing of love and beauty and truth. There must be more than imitations. So the bloom that comes from us must be an efflorescence from the living root that God planted in our nature. I know this will be nothing but a human blossom in itself; therefore I add, that every soul which draws nigh to God in a way to acquire the Divine character, must have this human blossom *fertilized* by the counter-bloom of the Divine nature itself. The human is the candle, but it must be lighted by the Divine spark. The human, however pure, is nothing more than the measure of meal; it must be pervaded by the Divine leaven. The human, however perfect in its stage, is still raw and unripe until perfected by the clime far away. This is the way character comes; this is the manner of it and the substance of it.

It is evident, therefore, that no more external institute, ritual, ordinance, can ever bring a spiritual, ethical being to the spiritual, ethical standard of another being; no ecclesiastical status can put a soul into proximity to God; no dogmatic furnishings, however full, however fiery, however ancient, mossy or recent, have anything to do with this. It is a matter personal, entirely; it is a matter spiritual, essentially; it is a matter of character, quality of soul, intensity of virtue, and only this. It means sweetness and purity of heart, of spirit, of temper; it means Christliness of soul; it means Godliness of character; and that is all it means.

Now for exactly this you must see that Jesus

Christ came into the world bringing his grand Gospel. Christ and the power of God in his teachings, are here to draw men unto Him. They are to draw men up, not to drag God down. Christ and his Gospel are the long arm of the Almighty reached out to the world. They brought the Father within feasible, visible reach of the child. Christ told the world the way to God; furnished the world the truth towards God and the life of God. He told men how to go to Him, and what to do, to be, to suffer and enjoy, as they should rise in character to the Divine standard. Christ and his teachings were the spark to light the candle; they were the pollen scattered from the heavenly blossom upon the human bloom of our human nature; they were the leaven in this measure of meal, making bread for angels. And all this was and is a provision for every solitary soul of the world; light for every man, bread for every child of the race; hope for all who will yield the due measure of confidence and trust towards God. Not for mankind only — all peoples and climes and kindreds of this world — but for other worlds, too, is this gift of Christ and his teachings. Included therein is an organic function by which the fortunes of two orders of existence are woven together. We are in the planting hour; we are to be in the reaping hour by and by. Such organic unity is stipulated and vouched for by Christ and his Gospel, sent into the world by God to tell us of this great and glorious thing.

Now, exactly here are the meaning and worth of

all religion; here is the meaning and the reality of salvation. To be saved is to become like Christ — like God — not in your talk, not in your ceremony, not in your imitation, not in your symbols, but in your virtues, in your *character;* and just in the *degree* that you come near to the high standard, are you saved. As you come short you lack salvation. Some are scarcely saved — saved as by fire. Some will be but as a glimmering, twinkling speck, while others will be like radiant stars; and others still, according to the Book, like burning suns in the canopy of glory. Just in the ratio under which we stand in our character to the Divine character, will be our status in the world of life.

What a glorious conception this is! What a grand scheme of being to contemplate! How the mere thought of it seems to throb down its inspiration into brain and all nature! The glory thereof becomes an anticipative glow and charm in the human heart. What waking under the inspiring touch of the glorious conception that we live and move and have our being under such grand economy as this! Beginning to exist as an image, and environed by Divine and immortal helpers, our growth and development reach that final, terminal stage, in which we shall stand completed, answering face to face unto God.

There have ever been *two opinions* in the world respecting this matter of religion and salvation. One has been, that man should come to God; the other has been, that God should come to man. Now I think that we may steer clear of difficulty by the light of our subject. God has already come to man in Jesus Christ; in his Gospel; in the revelations of all his providence; in the revelations of all his works. He has already come, and is here, in the possibilities and in the provisions of salvation. Man must come to God in the actualities of these possibilities — in the realization of these provisions. He is to make concrete what before was only in the abstract. He is to make substantial what was at first only shadowy and hypothetical. God *has* come, and man has *to* come.

Again: it has been the opinion of a portion of mankind, that God was to do everything and man nothing; while on the other hand, the opinion has been, that man is to do everything and God nothing. Now the light of our subject scatters all such confusion. The God of heaven did indeed let down the golden ladder whose foot touched to the uttermost the depths of humanity, and then the call was, "O man, ascend this ladder and draw nigh unto me; for in such ascension I shall be nigh unto you." We are co-workers with God. Those notions I just referred to were not born of the New Testament; they were born among the musty speculations of cloisters; they are a kind of hybrid offspring from the wedlock of pagan philosophy and the sweet gospel of St. John. God created us in his likeness, with the possibility and capacity of reaching his own substance, his virtues through our fidelity. There was his work, and here is ours; and this confusion vanishes. Hence that grand passage in Paul: "Work out your own salvation with fear and trembling." These institutions, these positions, these motives and grand inspiring labors working in you, in all your endeavors to do God's command, namely, to come up to the standard of His character. The nearer you work to this standard, the nearer you will be to Him; the nearer you agree with God, the more directly does He agree with you; and when you come together, that oneness is peace, reconciliation, atonement realized.

I want you to think of that word atonement. It is not a sounding syllable; it is not a mere passing word; there is unspeakable depth of meaning in it. It means the bringing of the soul into fellowship, harmony and union with God; renewing it after his own divine likeness; filling it with his own wisdom and unselfish love; bringing it *at one* with Him in feeling, desire and purpose.

The value of Christ and his religion is exactly here: *God's power to bring humanity, as to its character, up to the standard of Divinity, as to its character.* Christ and his character are virtue-powers to make men virtuous; they are holy powers to make us holy; they are Godly powers to make us godly; heavenly powers to make us heavenly. Not substitutes — not mere cards of presentation — they mean ourselves, or Christ's spirit and character in us.

Just in proportion as we approximate, morally and spiritually, the Divine standard, the difference between that standard and ourselves vanishes. When our souls are ripened into the fullness of the heavenly fruition, we shall be fruits of immortality; and in such coming to God, He will have come to us in oneness and ripeness and sweetness forever.

Here is the great Reconciliation; yes, the great Reconciler. They stand as the pledge that whosoever worketh in the name of the Lord and in the nature of the Lord, shall not find his work in vain. They come down here as the ascending path of man up to glory; and we walk step after step, step after step, as we add virtue to virtue, grace to grace.

Mistake not times and places — not this mountain or that mountain, not this church or that church, not one denomination or another denomination — for God. *Wherever* there is a spiritual, devout heart or character, there God is tented and there heaven begins.

The time for all this is life — the long life we may live on earth; every day, not one-seventh of the days; not special places and times and seasons alone, but continuous life; the deeds of men, the thoughts of men, the motives and beliefs of men in their current birth and flow. Not only must we be *sometimes* drawing near to God, but *always;* when we buy, when we sell; when we speak of each other; when we patrol the streets alone or in company; when we are at a neighbor's house; when we are the custodians of his reputation or his character. We are always drawing near to God, or increasing the distance between ourselves and Him. Not only in our doctrine; not only in our creeds; not mainly in our ecclesiastical status; not solely in our professions; but essentially in *ourselves* do we draw near to Him.

Time is drawing us near to God. The golden hours are singing of Him. We are approaching Him; we are nearing the tribunal where we shall see Him in his character. Then in the light of it we shall see truly our own. The question I ask now is, Will it be a burning·contrast, or a sweet resemblance? Will it be a jarring discord, or the chime which makes the key of eternity's song? We are nearing God in this sense rapidly. He will not ask us about human standards. There will be no question put as to whether you conform to this standard or that or the other, remotely laid down or recently. Not a word will be said about such things. Here is the standard, divine, immortal; God himself, only God. "How square you unto that, O soul? How much are you like Me?"

"O Lord, have we not taught in thy name, sung in thy name, fought in thy name? have we not burned heretics in thy name? have we not turned the world upside down in thy name?" "I never knew you," may possibly be the only response; "how much are you *like* Me?"

The fruits of the spirit are sweetness, gentleness, love, purity, power, grandeur and glory of soul, fragrance of saintliness that shall make angels ask for the regaling of your presence, if you are thus fruitful.

There is a beautiful world over there — beautiful as God, populated greatly already. Thousands of harps are struck by fingers we have pressed. They are triumphant; they bear the likeness. What, O soul, is your great interest as you draw nigh to that world? Will they greet you gladly? Will old sundered loves strike hands of recognition again, like music melting into music? That is all a matter of fitness; all a matter of virtue, sweetness, charm — of how much you are worth in God's sight, as related to their worth in his sight.

We are coming not only to God, nearing not only the spiritual world, but we are nearing our final self, our second self, the terminal self. We are nearing the self of harvest, of which the present hour is the seed-planting. Shall we be glad to see ourselves? Shall we be a benediction upon our own heads for ever and ever? Will there be peace in here — at heart? will there be power here, and shall I be easy-mannered in heavenly presences? Will my mien and spiritual bearing be that of homelike grace in the society of beauty and blessedness?

These are the questions to ask now. If we are drawing near to the significance of things in this sense, then we shall be saved. We need have no other thought, in faith, in prayer, in deed, in memory or hope, but this identity of worth with God — this at-oneness or union of our souls with Him. Draw near to Him, then, in truth, in purity, in beauty, in blessedness; accord with Him in his estimate of the nobility of true humanity; glow with Him in the fervor of an immortal and unselfish love; and this shall be spiritual and eternal nearness.

So come back to the mansions, the household of heaven; so dwells for ever the Father with the children.

XVII.

THE LAMBHOOD OF GOD—AND HOW IT TAKES AWAY SIN.

Behold the Lamb of God that taketh away the sin of the world. — John i. 29.

THE word *lamb* is a prominent Bible word; and as we find it in connection with altar usage, together with the tropical sense which it bears in the imagery that sets forth the Divine nature, it is so familiar and well understood that it is not needful to tarry for formal elucidation. All that is tender and gentle is implied; all that is pure, patient and long-suffering in God is intended. It means God's self-sacrifice; his suffering sensibility in view of sin; his distress at our self-inflicted injuries; his grief and burden of love over our unfilial dereliction, and his unrequited love. In a word, it signifies God's heart pierced by our transgressions, and bearing the load of our sins and our guilt. His soul-sympathy weighed down for us; wounded, weeping, sorrowing love; the great self-compensating balance of his own nature, whereby sorrowing paternity begets a tribute to Deity itself, and the capability of self-sacrifice in the interests of redemption from sin and disaster, stands as innate satisfaction from the foundation of the world. Such is the *Lambhood* of the Divine nature.

The Lamb of the Old Testament is typical, symbolical, ceremonial, lustral; the Lamb of the New Testament is personal, spiritual, real; the Lamb of God is living, loving, divine, eternal.

There is the sign; there is the word; and there is the idea. In the Old Testament it blossomed; in the New it fruited; but the root or seed was in God, and *was God*. Sublimely may it be said: "In the beginning was this Lambhood, and the Lambhood was with God, and the same was God."

Men are accustomed to say, the *Fatherhood* is God; the *Christhood* is God; the *Lambhood* is God; the *Spirithood* is God, putting predicate for subject. Say, better, the Fatherhood is *of* God; the Christhood is *of* God; the Lambhood is *of* God; the Spirithood is *of* God — using, as the grammarians say, the *subjective* genitive instead of the *objective*.

Fatherhood, Christhood, Spirithood, do not locate their meaning *outside* of God, objective to Him; but *inside*, carrying only a subjective significance. They interpret God; tell what *He* is, not what something else is. They are of Him; reveal Him; are Himself speaking, working, creating, re-creating. There is that true of God which gives divine fitness to such diction. He thus becomes his own dictionary.

Taking this view of the matter, the way is clear and direct to certain results. If God is the Fatherhood of the world, then this Fatherhood is divine and eternal; if He is the Christhood, then the Christhood must be divine and eternal; so if He is the Lambhood, the Lambhood must be divine and eternal, slain from the foundation of the world. The same is true of all that may be justly predicated of the divine and eternal Godhood. Thus the Divine Nature stands in unbroken coherence from the foundation of the world; in organic oneness from first to last, whether contemplated in relation to Creation, Providence, or Redemption. God is One; his government one. His mighty scheme of wisdom, love and power is but Himself projected; an organic whole of vital functions, holding sovereign unity in correlate diversity and subordinate manifoldness as essential to the absolute unity. In *Him* do all things consist.

The Lambhood of God is the heart of God; that cherished inmost that lies in the bosom of the Father, innocent, tender, gentle, patient, yearning, long-suffering, self-sacrificing, bleeding, interceding. It is this sorrow-pierced, sin-bearing, heart-aching stress of Paternal passion, whose *innate necessities* are fitly pointed to in the symbol, naked of euphemism, "slain from the foundation of the world."

We know, then, *where to look* for our Christ, the Lamb, the Gospel and salvation. They are of God, in God, yea, are God himself. To seek them elsewhere is to be *a*-theistic in our religion.

We are thus able to be sure of our standing firmly and clearly on *Monotheism*. We have not gods many, but one God, besides whom there is none other. This truth was the sublime assertion of the Old Dispensation; not less sublimely asserted in the New, but more fully developed there, and brought, executively, into adaptation to the life, nature, and necessities of man. Damaging constructions of this central truth of all true religion, through the refracting glasses and glosses of Pagan theology, have been at the foundation of most of the confusion in Christian theology, bringing strife and mournfulness to many. To depart from Monotheism, is to enter Polytheism.

From the premises laid down, the *Divinity of the Gospel* is not only an easy but an inevitable inference. Whatever is of God or Godhood, be it Creatorship, Fatherhood, Christhood, Lambhood, or Spirithood; be it mind or heart; be it law or love, it being *of* God, and so far forth God Himself, is necessarily Divine. And this Divinity from the fountain-head, is all that our humanity in its several phases of want, needs to perfect it. They twain make one new man.

Nobody, then, can doubt the *eternity of the Gospel* if it is *of* God, a native wealth and competence of His being. The element of time does not appear in the origination of the Fatherhood, Christhood, Lambhood of God; they only eventuate in time. To make the Christian gospel less ancient than God, is to drop it out of the category of the supernatural and divine, leaving it only a bubble on the passing stream of phenomena.

Here we touch the *unity* of the Gospel. The whole moral government of God, nay, his universal government is one. Its Christ, its Lamb, its Spirit, its Paternity, all one — coherently, concurrently one; a vital, organic, harmonious whole; with no conflict, discrepancy, or incompatibility of functions, interest, purpose or tendency, from first to last. The end was in the beginning, and the beginning was competent to the end; and there was no intermittent pulse between them, no mended link or remedied defects. It is a grateful consideration, as inspiring as it is true, that no regulator had to be introduced into the Divine government from foreign sources, the regulator being in and of the government to begin with. It is a stimulating challenge to love and trust, that neither God nor his government can come to any dead centres which they cannot pass without the aid of some additional momentum introduced to enable them to proceed. God, in the organic premises of his nâture and government, is all-sufficient and cannot be reinforced. Christianity is a divine anticipation in the nature of God, looking to the necessities of man.

Of course the *sufficiency* of the gospel is too evident to be made plainer. Its adequacy is in itself; its measure is its origin. The adequacy of God is that of his gospel. Does it not transcend all human necessity? Can the Infinite and Eternal be mended in his own necessities? Can He be helped save as He helps Himself?

Here is the great challenge to *Faith*. Confidence cannot be misplaced or betrayed. The strength of it is in the pillars and beams of the universe; the foundations of it, eternal Love. Here *Hope* roots. Its strength of expectation and desire draws nurture from the depths of Deity. Its bloom shall never wither; its fruit will be immortal. Here is *heart*. Man can take up the great problem of existence with a sense that there is solid substance in it. He can approach God with a holy boldness; he can advance with a sublime audacity of confidence and trust. Courage breeds as it dares. Crowns brighten by the conflicts in which they are won. No greater salvation can there be, than to melt into this heart-fire of God. The Lambhood of God, become a passion in the soul of man, is the gospel heaven. No greater punishment can there be, than to wake up at last and find that it was not an iron-crowned despot, but this very Lambhood of God I struck at and resisted; this suffering gentleness and gentle patience that loved me, whose aching heart my sins pierced, and whose sin-bearing love I wounded with ingratitude and indifference. This Lambhood is the *Power of God* unto salvation. It is the God-power because it is the nature of God, original and eternal as his Being. He did not acquire it in addition to his native competence; no God or gods *ab extra* brought it to Him, or in any way contributed enabling considerations, or augmented his power to save. The power was already in Him; the ability was of Him and eternal; the competence could no more be aided or increased, than could the being of God itself. He was self-sufficient of Himself. God could express and apply this eternal competence of his nature to the nature of man; and this is the *whole matter of Christianity*. Revelation means nothing else. It is the forthputting, forthspeaking of the interior of God's nature, as a divine, vital power, for the purpose of propagating itself in man's nature and developing, healing and perfecting it in his own likeness. Of Him and from Him and through Him and to Him, are all things, to whom be glory for ever.

Having shown what the Lambhood of God is, I proceed next to show what it was and is *for*, or *how* it "taketh away the sin of the world." The final *end* of every revealed truth, determines, not outside of us, not in God, not in religion, but *in us*. And what is that end? Precisely this: *To make you and me and all God's creatures bearing his image, finally, in character, like Him.* That is the *end* and the *aim* and the *for* of the whole thought and scheme.

I remark, in the first place, that the Lambhood of God takes away the sin of the world by *entering into man*. The stand and status for operation are not extraneous to man; not in God; not in Christ; not in creation; not anywhere or anyhow exterior to man's nature itself. Directly *in it*, and only there, is the field of its operation and power.

And I remark in the second place that the Lambhood of God takes away the sin of the world by getting not only into man, but into his *very heart*, the vital centre of his being. This must be in order that the Divine power thus entering, may get into the vital circulation of our very existence; may flow wherever its blood flows; go wherever the vein or artery ramifies; that it may get into the very juices of our existence; may mingle with the generative sap of the very fibre and flavor of our character, the heart, the digestive and assimilative function of our nature.

And then I add, in the third place, that the Lamb of God takes away the sin of the world by *cleansing* the world. O, how should men ever have mistaken this? The very function we are speaking of is that of cleansing — actual cleansing. I mean the cleansing of persons, of individuals, of specific and actual hearts and minds and consciences and entire souls. I make this emphasis for the sake of distinguishing between what is actual and what is substitutional or hypothetical. The cleansing must be of *yourself*, and it will not help you to have anybody else cleansed. The whole force of the thought must hug this fact of personality.

How do you cleanse, for example, a stain on the pure white paper? How do you purge the dark vicious stain from the pure white linen? You ply the spot with a hidden yet vital and forceful chemical, until the paper becomes whiter and whiter, and at last is as white as snow. Thus with your pure linen; you *cleanse* it; and you give a great deal sometimes for the secret as to how this may be done, that the good thing thus damaged for the time may not be destroyed. Just so there is a divine chemistry in the heart of God throbbing itself out sometimes in tears and anguish, sometimes in the native stress of paternity, that gets into the heart and plies you there, and takes the stain of sin away. No substitution will do that; no faith in the chemical force of God's virtues simply will do it. The application of the force of the virtue must be direct and personal, irrespective of all substitutes.

How do you cleanse a diseased body? Your child is sick; your friend is languishing under the fell touch of poisonous infection; and what is your course? You take the medical prescription and put it into the very heart of life; you so administer it that it shall be distributed in the circulation and work its purifying mission in the blood, in the very juices of life; and thus your child becomes medicated and cleansed. You do not substitute somebody's life for the life of your child. You do not ask your child to look at the medicine, saying, "Child of my heart, have faith in that, and be healed." You want him to have faith in it of course; but that alone will not save him. You want him cleansed; you want the disease taken away personally, not hypothetically.

You will observe that it is a *moral cleansing* that the Gospel contemplates, not a material, physical or legal cleansing. You will further observe that it is not a *ceremonial* cleansing; not a symbolic cleansing; it is not the *play* of being made clean acted upon the stage, the observance of which as spectators or participants, is assumed to be sufficient — not that. You may do that to the end of your days, and grow in uncleanness.

But I add, in the next place, that the Lamb of God takes away the sin of the world by *toning up the moral powers of our nature*. Sin is abnormal; sin is disease. It is, therefore, taken away by so invigorating the normal functions and elements of our moral system as to foster convalescence, and enable it to so antagonize and resist sin, as successfully to throw it off. Without this concurrent nurture and development of normal resources, these capacities and susceptibilities created within us by God, wherein we stand constituted moral beings, the exclusive medication of abnormal conditions will never successfully take away sin. For debility is there, you understand, by nature. Long before any man sinned, he was capable of sinning. There was an "infirmity" in him that is "helped" by the Divine tonic. And what I want is, that man may have strength not in him by nature — whether by development, by discipline, by use or otherwise — so that sin may be taken away and kept away.

I add, further, that sin is taken away by *fructifying* human nature by a higher principle and life than naturally and normally adheres in it; I mean the life and principle of the Divine nature; in other words, the Lambhood of God. This is very important.

You know how it is in the analogies of nature. It is not good for one element to be alone. The floral world tells us how it is that a single flower left by itself, is a barren thing; it will bloom and waste its sweetness on the air, and bear no fruit until it is fertilized by a counter-bloom. That is what our humanity wants. Even if it had never sinned, it wants that to keep it from sin; but having sinned, much more does it need this high and new fructification in order that strength may be generated within it to resist the assaults and successes of sin.

All may be summed up in this one grand word: The way to take sin away from the world as well as to keep it away, is, to *propagate the nature of God in the naturehood of man.* To generate the character of God in the character of man, is regeneration. Then the status of our humanity becomes that of Divinity, and we are saints of God indeed.

Here a double action is inaugurated: that of assault and attack against sin; and that of nurture and stimulation of right, goodness, holiness. Man needs to be stimulated, fed and encouraged, as well as to extend the theatre of conflict wherein sin is exterminated and driven from the field. For when right dethrones wrong, wrong is exiled from the realm of the conflict and sin is taken away. When the old character is driven out by the expulsive power of the incoming new character, then a new nature ensues, and sin is so far removed. Just as fast as the Lambhood of God ingenerates itself in the naturehood of man, man is purged and sin is taken away — not theoretically only, but actually. Theories of themselves won't do us any good.

So far as an unjust man is made just, he is justified. The meaning of the word *justified* is, *made just.* God never justifies a man while he is in the wrong; because while in the wrong God cannot approve of him, and He cannot justify what He does not approve. His wrong must be driven out of him; and the power to drive it out and take it away and make him righteous, is in God, "from the foundation of the world." It did not have to be put into Him some time afterwards. And when that God-power is used by man, and becomes through his fidelity a power of character in him, then his sin is taken away. Now God can approve of him; now He can justify him; for man thus conforms to God, the ever just and true.

So men are sanctified as far as the sanctity of God pervades and purifies their life and character. I know many are sensitive about these words, life and character. How beautiful are the feet of those who come upon the mountain with good tidings. The beauty depends upon the height; distance lends enchantment to the view. But let the feet of the prophet tread the valleys where sin lives, and apply his fiery message with "Thou art the man," and the salutation is very different. "Away with him! Away with him! Crucify him!"

Men are *redeemed* — actually, I mean, not substitutionally — when the power of redemption becomes enthroned in their nature, dethroning the power of sin and destruction, or taking it away. Redemption means getting a man out of wrong; but to get him out of wrong is only to get wrong out of him. There is no other possible way to rectify him.

Thus we see what the great *Reconciliation* of the Gospel is. God is in Christ, reconciling the world unto Himself; that is, harmonizing its character to his own character. Man is reconciled to God when he reciprocates God's reconciliation from the foundation of the world to him. That is, when the soul within us reciprocates that love which first loved us, then the great chord of God and man is struck, and the music of reconciliation begins.

Exactly so with *Atonement.* How men haggle with this word, and much more with the idea! They bandy it from Dan to Beersheba, as we kick a football in a game. Many times they don't know the first meaning of it. They use it as a kind of talismanic charm or mystic sorcery in the play, wherein they exercise their faith and hope of heaven. Let us see. The power of atonement is the power of the Lambhood of God; the Lamb nature of God. When that power, therefore, becomes an executed fact in your moral nature, transforming that nature, through your fidelity, into a new character, then your sin is atoned for and actually taken away. Otherwise it remains in you. You may formulate your theories of atonement till you are tired; they will not touch your character until the power of atonement enters you as a character-creator, taking away your wrongness and putting in its place, or helping you to put in its place, that which is right and true and pure. Atonement objectively considered, that is, as it stands stated in God, is simply the *heart power* of God, to be let into your heart like a life-stream to make you pure and sweet and holy.

The washing of *regeneration* we read of right here in the Book, is a grand and glorious idea. But it is not a washing outside of man; it is a washing *inside* of him, or it will not benefit him. A washing of regeneration, or anything else that leaves man's character just as it was before, is a mere mockery.

It is the juggler's game, or the game of the dupe. The washing that God means is a washing that takes hold, cleansing the man's character, making it clean and pure and righteous. No matter how orthodox your theory of the Divine "soap and water" may be; the only orthodox question about the matter is, How clean are you? How clean? How thoroughly rubbed and scrubbed and rinsed out are your life and character, by this cleansing power before God? "Blessed are the pure in heart for they shall perceive God." The grand Gospel of our souls is not some sublime or divine washing-machine, to be praised and glorified in grandiloquent way, as if that would make one white; as if that would save us. Our characters need to be fomented and fulled and bleached by the detergent vitality of truth and love. The grand Gospel is a stream of chemical divinity that must pour itself through us, and drench us through and through, or our sins will not be washed away.

O, thousands upon thousands are there who would much rather ride into heaven upon the shoulders of some substituted sin-bearer, than forsake their own sins and foot it for themselves by way of the Sermon on the Mount. How much more eagerly would they cling to that proxy way of being saved, than hold themselves responsible to that moral code which steers clear of sin, and helps God to get it out of them. This is the reason why thousands upon thousands who are often called Christians, seem at last so unwashed, so uncleansed. Praising the Fountain of salvation don't save anybody. The great question still comes, How clean has that Fountain made you as to your life — your character? There the matter stands and will stand, and hugs us closely. No wonder we want to shake it off. No wonder that proxy faith sometimes says, that putting Christ directly into the soul in this searching personal manner, is a "departure from the Gospel." It *is* a departure from *their* Gospel.

Be it remembered that the Lambhood of God—the Christ of God — did not come into the world simply to make money for us that we may be idle, and in our idleness steer clear of the disadvantage of bankruptcy. The power of God in his Lamb or his Christ, came into this world to tell us how we may make money for ourselves, and *so* lay up the treasure of heaven. "Thou oughtest therefore to have put my money to usury," said Divine Wisdom. "Thou oughtest to have made the five talents ten," was the condemning rebuke administered to the primitive Antinomian. Trusting to Christ, with Christ left out of life and manhood and womanhood and character, is substitution indeed; but the substitution is that of the word for the thing meant.

Two theories have held the world in division from the first. One holds that the Gospel tells us of the Divine goodness, purity, holiness and righteousness which God takes and substitutes for our goodness, purity, holiness and righteousness; and on the ground of this substitution, assumes to save us irrespective of our works. The other holds that this same Divine goodness, righteousness, purity, holiness is not a substitute for our own qualities and character, but a God-power to create these very qualities and virtues *in us*, and thus make us meet for heaven. Between these two you must choose.

The first is the *speculative* view of the Gospel; the second, the *practical*. The first is the *scholastic* view; the second, the *Biblical*. The former is the legal conception; the latter, the moral and spiritual. One is the symbolical and ceremonial and ritual view; the other is the ethical, real, actual, personal, vital view. The first-named holds that faith alone saves without works; the last says that faith is good for nothing except it be substantiated and proved by works.

Hence the corresponding division upon the whole matter of human responsibility. Both, you know, quote the passage, "Work out your salvation with fear and trembling;" but while on the one hand it is held that God is supposed to take hold of man by absolute power, just as you may hitch your team to the plough and drag it through whether it will or not; on the other hand it is claimed that God and all that is revealed of Him coming into contact with us, acts as a vital inspiration, as a vital motive-power upon us, whereby all our dormant powers and sleeping capacities are roused into action, and so man is put upon conscious endeavor Godward in his own behalf. Both quote this other passage, "Without me ye can do nothing." They are the words of Christ; but while one holds that Christ uses man, assuming to take him up in his arms and carry him along passively, without any endeavor on man's part; the other holds that man must use Christ, or the power of God in Christ, as a help, laying hold of Him, as it were, the power of eternal life. Man must use these Divine helps, without which he can do nothing, that they may stay his infirmities and become strength in place of his weakness, enabling him to do what without them he could not do. It is a glorious consolation, that God does not require us to do anything without that help; but it is an equally strong and irrevocable truth, that that help being given, we shall accomplish nothing unless we use it.

Here is where we come into the grand co-operation. Paul speaks of men as co-workers with God. Here God's heart works, turns, labors towards us, in order that it may wake ours responsive to it; a grand reciprocity of human and Divine action and life, taking away sin. Divine inspiration throbbing down out of the very Lambhood of God into human hearts, that aspiration may be born and love be awakened, reciprocating the love that first loved us — this regenerates and saves.

The whole matter of these two opinions, these two modes of thinking of the Gospel, standing opposite each other, may be summed up thus: One holds that the Gospel of Christ is of no advantage to man, any further than that gospel is in him changing his character from wrong to right, from stain to purity, from weakness to power, from impotence to high strength; of no sort of use touching salvation outside of man

— but must come *inside* of him, and be a reality in his personal character. That is one view. The other view leaves out of the question human works and human character, and looks upon salvation as something executed outside of man's nature, in God, in his government or Christ; holding that this Divine work and righteousness thus provided, are to be substituted in place of man's works and righteousness; and on this ground man is to be saved. This is the other view. Or briefer still: One presents the Gospel as a power to create in man a heavenly character; the other regards it as offering a substitute for such character. So much for the difference.

This, then, is the application of the Lambhood of God to the wants of mankind, and the practical development of its economy in the sphere of human nature. Thus as moral beings we are brought into grand concurrent action with God, and the true idea of the Gospel problem is stated.

And how beautiful all this seems! How like the charm of a benediction it comes down from the skies and beyond the skies, upon our parched and needy earth of humanity! What grandeur, what far-reaching scope of wisdom, love and power, from the foundation of the world! Fearful stress of the paternal heart, native to that heart, throbbing out in time to touch you and me, waking responsively the filial tear, the filial repentance, the filial love, that the child and the Father may be one again! This beauty of life, this forceful searching virtue of God pervading man's nature and purging the very texture thereof, how genial, how beautiful, how hopeful! O, where is the faith that will turn away from this to dream of a better?

For it is no dry externalism, you see; it is no dry, heated, fiery legalism; but the mellow summer of God, all dripping with dew upon the very expectancy of our native bud and bloom, to bring it forth to fruit and perfectness.

God is no hard master put in this way — O no. He never appears a hard master when we ask the New Testament for Him, or the Old one when we get down beneath the letter; for He is all the time sending the rain upon the unjust as well as the just, starting in us intelligence and hunger; suffering our very dereliction, our very ingratitude, our very sins even, that we may finally come to right and truth and love.

If you sin, O soul, you do not sin in an economy of government that dooms you to disaster in the premises; there is a second opportunity for you. If you sin, don't tarry long over your sin; all you need in your heart is, just to feel that grief which your sin has created in the heart of God. Your sin does not sting Him to rage; your sin does not unsheathe the flaming sceptre of his fury; it breaks the tear fountain of his nature — that very nature which I mean by the Lambhood of God the Father.

This is the deep, vital, gentle power that is working wonders in the world. At first the world was hard, crude, undeveloped; and it could not make much show. God had to handle it with a rough share. But Providence is mellowing the soul of humanity; this gentle tear-life of God is working at the very roots of the world, and throwing up beauty and sweetness and bloom. Why, don't you know this is just the way God is making the second Eden? And when He gets the spiritual Eden — the new Eden — done, no serpent will whisper there; no frailty will discrown manhood or soil the charm of womanhood. That will be the Paradise Confirmed. Unto that all this Gospel economy is tending. That is what it is all for; that is what it all means.

Trust in God, then, O soul. Give your heart to his heart. If He makes it ache and weep, your earthly father did the same when you were a child; and when manhood's years came, O how you thanked him for the strong hand and the severe rein!

There is no favoritism in this world of God; there is no partiality or respect of persons. Sorrow is for the whole world and for the sins of the world. The gates are open to all the world; whosoever accepts, passes in; whosoever scorns, he alone must bear it; there is no excuse; every lip is sealed.

Thank God for life in such a world, in such a government. Thank Him for the glorious outlook into a world that shall be cloudless, tearless, deathless. Thank Him when you have heart-aches that are throbbing out by a kind of stressful maternity, the birth of these higher revelations and restorations, the coming back of those confidences committed to God in the dark hours. Thank Him for the mend-ing of the broken chains, and for the re-living of the withered flowers of beauty and charm. Thank God for these, and for the depths of faith that can receive and appropriate them, and for the Gospel that gives this right.

For every beauty that shall retint the faded skies of life; for every flower that shall blush again upon its parched pathway; for every lamp that shall relume its chambers of night and silence; and for every crowned victor that shall spring from its graves, thank Him; and by the gift become like the Giver.

From the Lambhood of God that taketh away the sin of the world, shoots up the great exultation:

> See Truth, Love and Mercy in triumph descending,
> And Nature all glowing in Eden's first bloom;
> On the cold cheek of Death smiles and roses are blending,
> And Beauty IMMORTAL awakes from the tomb.

XVIII.

CHRISTIANITY AND HER FOES.

> *Heaven and earth shall pass away, but my Word shall not pass away.* — Matth. v. 18.
> *A man's foes shall be they of his own household.* — Matthew x. 36.
> *God hath made us able ministers of the New Testament, not of the letter but of the spirit.* — 2 Corinthians iii. 6.
> *He that hath not the spirit of Christ, is none of his.* — Romans viii. 9.
> *If this counsel or this work be of man, it will come to naught; but if it be of God, you cannot overthrow it.* — Acts v. 38, 39.

CHRISTIANITY ever since its birth, has had its so-called foes. There has always been a great deal of anxiety about its fortunes. Men stood in fear and trembling with respect to it before Celsus, Porphyry, Julian, and hosts of others attacking it externally. Even Paul himself was branded as a heretic opposed to the true faith. Look a little at this matter of solicitude.

A great and leading foe, spotted as opposed to Christianity, is and has been called *Science*. Paul speaks of this. But what he had in mind by science in that day, was, of course, the science that existed then; the speculations and philosophical theories of men. True science had not yet been born. Therefore we feel in this day at liberty to say, that neither religious nor any other truth, is in any peril whatever from *true science*. For true science is the thinking of God. While false science, like every falsity in the thinking of man, is sure to dispose of itself. All lies are harmless in the end. For like a combination of factors, one of which is a cipher, the product is frustration — nothing.

Another great enemy, which is and has been feared, is called *Rationalism*. I know these names are used as nick-names mainly; but then a careful observer of the human mind understands that a nick-name is all the stock in trade which a great many have. It is, fact, logic and devotion combined. It exhausts their methods of warfare; it exhausts their resources generally. Truth, whether religious or any other, has never anything to fear from reason — never. Reason in us helps to make the image of God; it is the organ his intelligence holds converse with. The great thing to be feared just here is not reason but *un*-reason — the lack of reason; the darkness which its luminous orb should replace. My people are destroyed from lack of knowledge, said the Prophet; and that is what every true prophet has said in this earth. The great thing to be feared is, not this grand function of God in the world, but its broken half; reason with one wing, with one foot; reason as a cold dead taper snuffed out, or carried about unlighted in the world. Thence come the blind leading the blind.

Another reputed foe has been christened *Doubt* or *Scepticism*. What does that word mean? *Skeptomai*, a Greek word, means to inspect, to examine, to carefully scrutinize any matter presented, as to whether it is worthy of credence or not. This kind of doubt is the balance of credulity; a pausing for evidence; a *demand* for evidence. This questioning is the only safeguard against superstition and cheat. Did you ever think that no man ever believed anything with more strength than he doubted the opposite? Did it ever occur to you that every action of your mind, when your credence is challenged, exercises itself under a double-poled function? If you come to the fork of the road, just in proportion as you believe the right to be the true way, you doubt the left. If you listen to the different statements made by two men on the same matter, just in proportion as you doubt one you believe the other. Doubt is as good a thing as faith, if you are careful as to what it refers. You had better doubt the devil than believe in him. You had better doubt a lie, than have faith in it. Yet men who follow the trade of jugglers have used this word "doubt" as a scarecrow, and called men sceptics who only doubted the divinity of the assailants' profession. The very first thing Christianity did in the world, was to challenge inspection from all minds, commanding them to search its authorities, even the very documents that assume to hold it and vouch for its genuineness.

Another foe has been named *Infidelity*. Well, this word has a meaning — a strong meaning. But always when you use it or hear it used, ask yourself to what it is referred. Infidelity means disloyalty, unfaithfulness, disbelief. But I had infinitely rather be infidel towards a falsehood, than to become a believer in falsehood. I had vastly rather.be unfaithful towards wrong, than to be faithful to it. It depends always upon what you are talking about, and how you understand yourself. For myself, I never feel better than *sometimes* when I am called infidel — for then, at least, I am sure that I am in good company. Our reading has to go but a little way to find that some of the brightest, purest and noblest of Christian men on earth, have been branded as "infidels." You have but to go down into the Turkish Empire to find yourself and all Christendom branded as "infidel dogs." Of course, they are Arabs and Barbarians and Bedouins who say this; but they claim to be the only orthodox believers in the world. One of the brightest luminaries in the most famed theological seminary in the land, within our memory, was called an infidel because of some of his interpretations of the Bible. To determine whether a so-called infidel is a foe to Christianity or not, you must first understand clearly and distinctly to what the word is applied, who applies it, and *for what purpose.*

Again: *Worldliness*, or secularism, has been regarded as hostile to Christianity. Worldliness, technically and actually, has stood as the great anti-Christ of faith. God on one side, and worldliness on the other, makes the battle. But when we examine, it will appear an easy thing for any boy to cipher out, whether Omnipotence on one side will be likely to be overthrown by the weaker party on the other. Read the last passage I quoted from the Acts: "If

s

this counsel and this work be of man, it will come to naught; but if it be of God, ye *cannot overthrow it.*" One of the greatest evils Christianity has been obliged to suffer, has come from this scepticism of faith, this want of confidence by men in their own belief. The Romanist says, Protestantism is the great foe to Christianity. Protestantism replies, Romanism is the great destructive enginery against Christianity. And so the indictment goes on. But let us talk a little more directly and positively.

The *real* foes of Christianity are such as these: First, those who, whether inside the church or outside the church, insist upon making a *definition* of Christianity out of its *accidents;* those who insist that the very essence and foundation of this religion are to be found in the material, sensuous, and phenomenal aspects of it. If a man outside the church wishes to stigmatize Christianity, he will get up a definition of it, and make that definition out of what Christianity sloughed off a thousand years ago. And when he has made his definition he will say: "There is your Christianity. A man of straw; a bundle of old clothes; and what is it good for?" Give any advocate the privilege of making the evidence on the other side, and his case is an easy one. Under such an arrangement you don't want but one lawyer.

The inside enemy does the same thing — not, of course, with the same intent. He professes to be the friend of Christianity. But carving her definition out of her phenomenal aspects, her imperfect, mutable and perishing accidents, he is from his position a greater foe to her life, health, and growth, than all the outside enemies that have banded against her. *They* are open; *he* is disguised. Persecution never kills truth; false patronage is deadly. It buries the truth alive; incarcerates it; suffocates it; makes a mummy of it, a husk, a stone; and then says, On this rock I build. The inside enemy is in secret league with the outside enemy, which twain constitute the great Anti-Christ of the world.

Again: he is an enemy to Christianity whose *method* of handling it is such that the whole problem of Christian life, character, and culture, is made to consist in believing, observing and manipulating the external matters out of which the false definition was made. This kind of conventional industry, with implicit faith in it, is put in the place of Christ and his spirit in personal character. He who makes it a matter of salvation to swing with hooks in his back, count his beads, boast of his ancestors, or invoice his orthodoxy, makes the mistakes Christ came to correct. He puts the signs of the Zodiac in place of the year's work. He who manages spiritual husbandry in that way, is a foe to Christianity;—not so much intentionally, or with malice aforethought, as in blindness and falseness. He is her undertaker more truly than her disciple.

Another real enemy to Christianity is *Bibliolatry;* the worship of the Book, instead of the worship of the God of the Book. As you read the letter of your friend's heart, does your heart throb towards its ink and paper and seal? Or is the great substance and essence of the whole thing that *friend's heart?* You read the letter again and again, seeking its meaning. You call in another friend and ask him what this sentence or that phrase means; and you study it until, by and by, you get the whole. Then you can put the letter into the waste-basket, into the fire, and lose nothing, because the great thing it means is in you; and though heaven and earth pass away, that meaning will still abide. We want the spirit, the deep life of this Book. We do not want a sentence or a letter stricken out. Thousands of commentators are at work upon it, but no two of them agree.

And so you and I are driven, in our poor necessities, to give the verdict ourselves. And we feel at liberty to do that, because the great Word has said: "Let every man be fully persuaded in his own mind;" "If any man will do the will, he shall know the doctrine." I choose the heavenly Master, not the earthly masters; and so must you. Such is not only truth, but Christian truth; not only Christian truth, but Protestant truth through and through. And if we cannot read the full meaning of the Bible until we get into eternity, very well. I do not suppose we can — though a good many *seem* to have done it — *seem* to have sounded the whole matter, and to have laid it away as settled forever. But God is greater than all his words. Worship God, then, and not any mere word He has spoken. The letter killeth, while the spirit giveth life evermore.

Another real foe to Christianity is a *false conception of the Divine Government*. Men do not intend wrong in this; but when they find out the wrong, and still insist upon it, then they are perverse in purpose.

A false conception of the Divine Government, in the first place, lies in the implication that it were imperfect to begin with; that in the administration of that government, its very functions and operations might come to a dead-lock, by virtue of which that government could not go on until relieved and enabled to act by some *extraneous* aid coming to its rescue. Whereas the truth is, that that government was and is able and competent, from first to last, without any additional legislation, without any amendment or improvement in any sense. Such is the *true* conception. Hence, from the false conception, men have ever regarded Christ and the Gospel and Christianity as the means by which 'that government is secured, established, and its integrity maintained.

But still another false conception lies in assuming that the grand gift of Christianity contemplates *sin* and *only* sin in the world; nothing but mortal or moral sickness. Whereas the Gospel is the very staff of life — nutriment for the healthy soul, as well as medicine for the diseased. "I am the *bread* of life come down from heaven," says the great Provider. It is for stimulating growth as well as for curing sin and purifying from evil. We want the whole truth, and not the half only; and he is a foe to Christianity who smites her in twain, and would leave her thus half dead by the way.

Another false conception lies in the assumption that the Gospel of Christianity seeks to introduce a *Substitute* for purity and holiness, instead of the virtues themselves. The truth is, that the government of God contemplates and demands these virtues in each one of us, and gave Christianity as the *power* to create such righteousness and true holiness in us personally. It is no fiction, therefore — no complimentary card which the bankrupt may present at the exchequer of the skies, saying, Take this instead of what I owe. Why, the punctilious Frenchman acted upon better wisdom — for there was less profanation in it — when he approached the altar and dropped his card upon it, paying thus his respects to the Almighty and his duty. These, and matters like these, constitute the real, biting, damaging hostility to vital and essential Christianity.

Another foe is the *assumed antagonism* of Christianity and other truth. I say it is assumed, because it is a false notion that science and reason are hostile to this faith; incompatible with it; irreconcilable. They are all brethren of the same Father.

Still another false foe lies in the thought that *nothing but science* is religion; that the only religion a man wants is scientific truth.

Equally false is the foe who declares that there shall be *no science at all* about religion. All truth is fraternal with Christian truth. This is not a divided household in the kingdom of God or the kingdom of humanity. I said in the beginning that science is nothing but the thinking of God; and can you have any religion that disfellowships the thinking of God? One of the greatest curses that have left their blight on the religious world, is this divorce of Christianity from the light of reason and common sense; the putting out of the torch of science, the flaming stars, the glory of the emerald and the topaz about the throne, whose dim reflection is God's candle in the earth.

Now, with such a front presented as the *definition* of Christianity, do you wonder that the intelligence of mankind stands aloof from it, and is arrayed against it? With such a definition, do you wonder that God raised up Voltaires and Humes and the sharp critics of later times to pick the flaws? Do you wonder that in this age of the world men stand forth and protest against the whole "syllabus" of such presentation? Why, under this view you see science and religion arrayed against each other; God in nature and God in grace, God in astronomy, geology, Genesis and the soul, put into interminable conflict. Under such a conception of Christianity reason stands arrayed against it; civilization is against it; all progress and improvement dead against it; manhood ignores it, and God himself discards the whole thing. This false putting of the matter has made all the *real* infidels in the world. It has dwarfed pulpits, depopulated churches, and will continue to depopulate them just in proportion as it is insisted on. A man's old clothes are *not* the man; last year's almanac is out of date this year; the implements of husbandry that raise the wheat, and the stubble left in the field, are not the bread of life.

God made the human soul for truth; and although the soul may not fully understand the cheat and jugglery, there is yet something in man that will rise up in some sixteenth and nineteenth century, and utter the grand protest of instinct and inspiration against the cheat. This very truth-instinct has been the ground of all the heaving protests and all the reactions in the world — the swinging of the pendulum to and fro in the movements of mind and history. From such an assumed, authoritative deliverance of Christianity, carved out of the mere perishable aspects of it, a substitution of phenomena in the place of persistent life or the essential spirit and true principle of the thing, comes delusion and corruption. Of course there must be revolts. And heaven itself is becoming populated from the so-called infidels who make up this army of dissentients — and from heretics like Paul and sceptics like Luther.

So that we are obliged in all this push and pull of matters just to fall back upon the grand words of that old Pharisee — Gamaliel — for there was more light in the sunset of the old dispensation than in all these will-o'-the-wisps we have been speaking of around the swamps of the Christian ages: "If this counsel and this work be of man, it will come to naught; but if it be of God, ye cannot overthrow it." And there every soul may stand secure. You may as well battle the advance of the stars as battle any truth of God. It is only the man-part that is shifting and vanishing; the mere human aspect of the subject; the crude, imperfect instrumentalities; the early drapery and perishable phenomena. These will come to naught; these will pass away. And he who insists upon making a definition of Christianity out of them, makes it of fiction, of the dust of the tombs. He who would build the everlasting kingdom upon such foundation, builds upon sand; and the storm is on the way that indeed shall overthrow it. While what God builds shall rise, more and more resplendent without end.

Still men cry, peril! danger! Not a thousand years ago, in civilized England, the inventor of umbrellas was stigmatized as an infidel for interrupting the designs of Providence with regard to rainy weather; for when the showers fell it was evident God meant that men should get wet. Not long since the self-constituted censorship of godliness stigmatized the scientific man as an infidel, who brought that balm and God-gift into the world, *Anæsthetics*. By the aid of this, the most violent surgical operation can be performed, while pain is banished into dream-land. The design of Providence is, it was claimed, that if a man's limb must be amputated, it should ache; and the inventor frustrated that design.

Why, within our memory also, the introduction of the practice of vaccination to prevent such pestilences as ravage whole communities, was stigmatized as the work of the devil; because disease is, by its nature, made contagious by God, and man should not interfere with God's doings. The plagues of the Old World came under the same handling; and the men who sought to stay them, and stop them entirely, were charged with infidelity. It was a meddling with Providence. That kind of logic has always existed in the world; it exists still. Thousands of men and women, conscientious and amiable, but not reliable in stress of weather, have wrapped themselves in their superstitions and hid themselves when fear came; and still they hide.

Also, because of this very thing, many seek to work a kind of *contraband* trade. In times of trial, when the chaff is sifted from the wheat and driven away by the winds, they speculate in ignorance and superstition. When the fire rages and all things are perturbed, then they run up false flags, attempting to make grand gains; if not in cotton, as in war times, then in sectarianism always belligerent. They run up these flags or devices for the capture of wandering life and unsuspecting virtue on the seas. You do not wonder, then, that men observing these things, raise the question as to what, after all, there is in Christianity to boast of; whether there is anything of real value in it at all.

To that question I am glad to reply for one, by stating facts — simply *facts*. Here is a power that has stood for eighteen hundred years, phenomenally, technically announced, in Providence. It has stood forever and forever in the essence and significance of the thing itself. But as it has stood the vicissitudes and fortunes of human life thus far, and is stronger to-day than ever, this fact is a witness for it. I know it does not command the suffrage of a majority of mankind; but when you see what it has done while yet in its youth, compared with the hoary age of some other religions, there is a *fact*, and quite enough for you.

And here is another fact. You will find that Christianity is allied with the strongest nations of the earth. Wherever there is the most cultivated brain, the grandest civilization under law, and the noblest uplifting of man, there you will find the Christian religion. This is an additional *fact*.

As you interpret it, basing its certitudes not upon phenomena, but upon essence, upon spirit, upon enduring principles, you will find that the very heart-throb of Christianity, its deepest life and inspiration, are in harmony with the heart-throb of the constitution of Nature. Well might the old Pharisee say, though he did not fully comprehend his own grand words, "If this counsel or this work be of man, it will come to naught; but if it be of God, ye cannot overthrow it." Just so far as these profound theses of the Christian religion strike hands with the theses and laws of God in creation, it cannot be overthrown. Though heaven and earth pass away, it will stand. And if all we often say shall prove true at last, namely, that there is another world, another order and dynasty of existence, then even that grander scale and order may give place to a still higher, and yet Christian truth endure.

Another grand fact is: Not only does Christianity accord with the "constitution and course of nature" in the material world, but she accords better than any other religion with the constitution of human nature, with the soul of man and the law of his being. So that when we shall see all these grand chords striking from within and without, when world answers to world, when the whole tide of national progress, the triumphs of reason, the victories of science, and the grander prophecies of intuition and instinct, all wave aloft their signs of fraternal greeting, we need not be much alarmed or troubled that we are in this great enterprise, and that we strike hands with such fellowships and such certitudes. We may be peaceful; we may be powerful. And as the mere phenomenal aspect is brushed away, as the scaffolding shall be taken down stage after stage, and the mystic hieroglyphics interpreted, you will see that the mighty destiny of Christianity is in the nature of things — just where we have always put it; and that her glory towers up more majestic than temples made with hands, beyond phenomena, beyond time, to be eternal in the heavens. It is mightier than man, and man shall not prevail against it. It is wiser than man, so no genius of evil shall circumvent it.

I will tell you some *real* ugly foes to Christianity as well as to all truth; foes to light, foes to purity, foes to righteousness. *Ignorance* is one. Men are not always to be blamed for their ignorance, but it is always to be lamented. It is never a helping hand to truth. *Hypocrisy* is another. The gentle Nazarene, full of the fragrance of heaven, uttered no violent word save in one instance; and that was against *hypocrisy*, the masked presence that men act behind. Another is *Bigotry*. Bigotry — it is the whole man put into a Chinese slipper and kept there. It is a stint and stench upon the human name that makes man unpresentable wherever there is light; liberty or nobleness. Another real foe is *Guile*. Deceit is a liar; trickery is a pious fraud — secret, polished, vulgar, snake-like, hidden away and hissing out of darkness, ashamed of its own tongue and face and heart. If it has never been canonized, it certainly has been the chronic plague of religion.

Another ugly foe to Christianity is *Indolence* — apt to be coupled with ignorance, when it constitutes that contentment which says, "I don't want to know any more than I do; I would rather rest in things as they have been made to my hand, whether right or wrong, than take the trouble of investigating and making wrong right." Such indolence would sooner ship on board some old leaky, rickety craft, than pay the necessary cost of a safe transit on reliable bottoms — using the logic that thousands had gone over safely before. But indolence forgets that the worm has been at work ever since, and that it is time for that which is worn out to be "folded away." Navigation, however, lives and commerce lives; seas are spanned and continents are traversed—and will be more and more, though all the earlier rafts and hulks go to the bottom, and the footman and postilion are heard of no more.

Greed of power is another ugly enemy to a live Christianity; tyranny, despotism; the enthroning of one man over the brain and conscience of another; the demand of worship paid to man instead of God; taking leave and authority from a poor frail mortal, less respectable even than the suppliant, instead of acknowledging the Father in heaven alone. All these are enemies, and it were high time they were banished, having a name in the world only by the leave of memory and history.

We pause then in our review upon just this: He who hath the *spirit* of Christ is christly; he who hath the spirit of God is godly; he who hath the thought of God inwardly, is so far reconciled to Him. The gates of hell shall not prevail against the Gospel of God, against the Christian religion, so sure as the fundamental truths thereof were born from the brain and heart of the Most High.

And you, O soul, so far as you have the *spirit* of that Gospel instead of the *letter*, will stand. Just in proportion as you carve your thought and definition of Christianity out of the heart and thoughts of the Almighty, the gates of hell shall not prevail against *you*.

This whole matter is undergoing a rehandling; man himself is undergoing a readjustment as to it. Story after story of ancient scaffoldings are coming down; higher ones are thrown up; and the building steadily rises. Some think they can see its dome already glittering among the clouds. Have something, O soul, to put into that immortal edifice. Do not stake your all in the mere scaffolding.

Then, when the bells shall be ringing for the great convocation, when the grand orchestra shall be breaking out up there, your voice will not be missing; you will be among the victors and harpers. Though the storm rages to-day, and though the drift of time goes down-stream, in patience, in grand confidence and steadfastness, possess your soul.

XIX.

PERSONAL RIGHTEOUSNESS— THE RELIGION OF THE NEW TESTAMENT.

> *Verily I say unto you, among them that are born of women there hath not risen a greater than John the Baptist.* — Matthew xi. 11.

THAT is high testimony standing in exactly the words of Christ Himself. And yet it is added: "The least in the kingdom of heaven is greater than he."

This greatest born in time is designated as the herald Preacher, the Harbinger of the New Dispensation; the Forerunner of Christ.

First we find him upon the banks of the old historic river, the Jordan, preaching to the multitudes, and baptizing them in its waters. Prophecy for centuries had been foretelling a Voice crying in the wilderness "Prepare ye the way of the Lord;" and when this ancient utterance broke from the lips of the grim, austere prophet of the hour, prefaced by the words "*I am he*," it was not strange that omens should have attended his birth.

From childhood, in which he was said to have been "full of the Holy Ghost," years passed on — even a generation — during which he knew naught of the world but his desert life. There the plastic wonder of early years felt the moulding touch of the rude aspects around him. He became familiar with crag and den and wild beast; he communed with the stately stillness of mountains, the solitude of the wilderness and the silence of the desert sea. These were his tutors; these were God's fountains of inspiration and power.

In the fullness of his time he suddenly appeared on the stage of the living world, and, like a thunderclap from the still sky, broke upon men with the startling word, *Repent!* This was the keynote of his mission. His hour had come, and he was ready for his work.

Thence ensued the meeting with Christ, the baptism of the "Greater" at the hands of the less; and from that august moment in which the Old was handed over to the New, and the desert passed into the garden, the former began to "decrease," and the latter to "increase."

This was at a marked period of the world; a time of great commotion, distraction and drifting uncertainty. The Roman tread was everywhere, and everywhere hated. Formalism reigned, and had become a weariness to patience and a drag on the better nature of man. No voice of living prophecy had been heard for well-nigh five hundred years; hope was low and heart was heavy and life at stagnant ebb. Well might the word, *Repent!* startle and thrill the world's dull hour.

But in such Divine words of life-giving energy there is not only hope but *battle*. The end of the herald preacher was not a crown, but a prison and the official act of the executioner. The dissolute life of Herod felt the fire of the words of truth, and his wrath was kindled. The character and life of the corrupt tyrant could not bear the searching scrutiny of the Baptist's morality, and vengeance determined on his destruction. Had John the Baptist preached the old forms and ceremonies of bygone ages, the outlived notions of Moses and the patriarchs about herbs, meats, pots, pitchers, cups and phylacteries, his head had been safe enough. Herod could have danced with Herodius or her daughter, and been as pious as anybody. But, *Repent!* "it is not lawful that thou shouldst have her," was a scandal to his "*faith.*" Salvation by a religion that leaves out morality, is not peculiar to modern times. This was the sunken snag along the channel of the new river of life, against which the divinely-freighted argosy of John the Baptist struck and went down — for the hour. The hulk perished, but the cargo was a Divine seed, that floated upon the waters, and is giving bread to the world after these "many days."

John was not the Christ, but his usher; the one the acorn, the other the oak; the one the morning twilight, the other the risen sun; the one the vernal seed-time, the other the summer growth and the autumn harvest.

The next day after the Jordan meeting, these two, the Herald and the Heralded, parted — never to meet again. The Old gave its hand to the New, and the New answered back in hearty grasp. The one abdicated, the other acceded. The latent germ of ages had blossomed out into the summer of the great Divine Year, and henceforth *this* was to "increase," and *that* to "decrease." Retreating, retreating, fading, vanishing, rolls back the glory that has been; while that which is to be, is towering, advancing, culminating in splendor and power, as the ages unfold their drama. Roman dungeons are strong; tyrants and bigots have been mighty in the earth; but bigots and tyrants and assassins in the name of God, have seen their brightest day; for truth rolls on, mighty as God Himself, and her chariot bears the victors.

No greater born of woman! Wherein lies the pre-eminence?

1. The preacher had *something to say*. He was charged with a message; and, like Paul after him, "Woe is me, if I speak not." John was no "repeater;" no reciter of old paradigms; no retailer of venerable hearsays already well enough known. He had something of his own to say, fresh and living, given to him by God. This gave him a right to say it; nay, was a necessity laid upon him. This gives any man a right; and it is all the right of his commission to speak at all.

2. He knew *what* it was he was to speak — the grounds of it and the reason for it. He had pondered it in solitude; he had communed with it on the heights of silence and inspiration. His conceptions were clear, his purposes distinct, his convictions profound, his object definite, his ultimate designs comprehensive.

3. His thought was in *advance* of his time. This panoplied him as well as imperiled him. Because he thought and spoke for ages to come, he found himself out of harmony with the average thought of his time, as well as under its ban. But herein he was strong, also; and without this striking ahead, no man advances. His words thrilled with inspiration from ages unborn. By underground wires he was in communication with eras and evolutions that had not been bulletined along the accustomed ways of men. Hence his fitness as a herald. Thus histories are summed up in single lives in advance.

4. This man was fired with a deathless *enthusiasm*. This fire was born in him; it was fanned in his desert life; it glowed by the Jordan; it flamed among the people; it waxed before Herod; it quailed not in felon's dungeon; it is a glory and consuming power to-day. No life can be above stale mediocrity without this inward glow and passion called enthusiasm. Kindled from truth and eternal principles, it is "God in us." It is the root of all heroism; it made the herald preacher daring unto death.

5. This nourished the root of unflinching *fidelity;* it bred the passion of unapproachable loyalty; it consecrated the law of his mission as his only law; it made him able to take all consequences; and in the fires of death to link truth to immortal life. So he was surpassingly great in the world, peerless among those born of women.

The application of the ethical element in Christianity to human life and character is the key-note of the Dispensation. Repent! reform! are the words that introduced it; and as was the key, so is the song. Christianity may be preached as a theory or a rite, and trouble nobody; but Christianity preached as repentance and reformation, never failed to stir up the Herods of life; and never will. Life and character like to be unmolested. Men are prone to rely upon outside saviors as their substitute, making theories and beliefs responsible for all their shortcomings. Had John the Baptist preached this way, all the Scribes and Pharisees and Tetrarchs and Judges in Judea would have flocked around him. There would have been no execution, no prisons, no grumbling. Had Christ preached thus, there had been no cross and no victim. John and Jesus are one; the Sermon on the Mount and "Repent!" "Woe unto you Scribes and Pharisees," and "who hath warned you," are one gospel from two preachers, the Herald and the Heralded. Personal righteousness is the religion of the New Testament. Substitutions were learned from neither Jesus nor John.

But is the prison a finality? Is the Harbinger really dead? Christ comes the fulfillment of John; to-day is the fulfillment of Christ; and to-morrow will be the fulfillment of to-day. The seed away back in the beginning, blossoms and fruits all along the fields of the future. Religion, so far as it has any fitness to man, is designed to make the world better, nobler, truer, purer. Aside from this result, Christianity is no better than any other religion. Because of the laying of the hand directly upon life and character, tyrants have hated its power, and "substitutionists" have disparaged its morality. The Christs and the Gods that men have made, have been praised and worshipped and believed in and trusted vastly more, in all ages of the world, than the one God of Christ, and the one Christ of God. Who shall ascend into the hill of the Lord? was the Oriental cry. "He that hath clean hands and a pure heart," was the Divine answer. And men who have said it ever since have been stoned.

The herald Preacher fell; the heralded Preacher fell; they both went down; but the fall of both was for the rising of many. The acorn perishes; the oak lives for evermore. The planters are for the endless to-morrow. Truth is God's presence ever breaking, ever rending old limitations, bursting the husk in which it was planted — the prisons which hold it for a time. Around the silence of the tombs where the valiant sleep, crowns are shaping, and amaranths put forth the bud whose bloom shall never fade. Beneath old battle-fields, silent now forever, but over which tyranny and bigotry and vice once drove their triumphant chariots, songs of truth, purity, fortitude and love are now writing their scores for the final jubilee.

Be a herald then, O soul! — a herald of truth. Be a harbinger of a New Dispensation, and stand forth as the prophet of something better — vastly better than anything that ever has been. The conflict shall more and more be behind you; the jar and the tumult and the carnage thereof, shall retreat into deeper and deeper silence; while the glory shall loom up before you, waxing and rising in power and divineness.

For the stress of patience and the valor of truth, there are always fadeless garlands; for enthusiasm that is of God, and heroism born from beyond the fight, there are altars more than priestly, and crowns more than kingly. Manhood is royaler than sceptres; Womanhood, diviner than shrines or lustral waters. Beyond the dim haze that veils it now, in golden light and beneath skies of pearl there sleeps a Coronation Day for both.

Is there aught greater or grander in life than to be Heralds and Harbingers of that Day?

XX.

*A COMPARISON BETWEEN THE OLD DISPENSA-
TION AND THE NEW.*

> *From that time Jesus began to preach and
> to say, Repent! for the kingdom of
> Heaven is at hand.* — Matthew iv. 17.

THIS is designed to follow the sermon of last Sunday morning, as the summer follows the spring. That gave religion as it fell from the lips of the Herald Preacher; this, as from the lips of Him whom the Herald introduced.

"From that time began Jesus to preach and to say, *Repent!*" that is, after the time of preparation. As the Forerunner went into the desert by way of communion, thought, finding out where he was, what he was to do and how to do it, and then came forth and spake; so Christ retreated from the early hours of childhood, from the haunts of the people, from the usages of his nation, into obscurity. Even after his announcement by John the Baptist, He went into the wilderness Himself — into the desert — and there passed through an experimental preparation which is characterized in the New Testament as the "Temptation." It means trial, simply; that is what the word generally signifies in the New Testament. Paul says: "Count it all joy when you fall into diverse temptations" — trials, tests and proofs of ourselves. After "*that time*" came forth Jesus, and began to preach and say, "*Repent!*" taking the same text, taking up the very seed of his dispensation from the dispensation of John. Scarcely had the voice of the Harbinger died away, ere its resonant echo awoke as from behind the mountains, breaking in more incisive accent upon the listening world around. *Repent!* was the summons as if from the trumpet-lip of God. John and Christ preach one gospel.

If you will notice, just a moment, this word *repent* is compounded of a double significance. It looks backward and it looks forward. It signifies, first, Drop the sins of old and accept the *pœna*, the *re-pœna* or punishment — the root-meaning of which is to fine oneself, to tax, to mulct. This repentance is a powerful self-crimination, an acknowledged retribution. Then, secondly, the meaning looks ahead; it is *Reformation*, the bringing forth of fruits meet for repentance. First, get clear of the old difficulties and thralls of the past; then, go on and do the proper work of life and man; build up, reconstruct, rear the grand temple of which your very nature is the material — under a high, divine architecture, indeed, of which God Himself is the inspiration and the scheme.

After that primal announcement of Christ, we find Him immediately doing — what? Preaching that grand inaugural discourse, the Sermon on the Mount. There He begins to expand his mission introduced by the Forerunner. He opens in those Beatitudes, so full of beauty and divineness: "Blessed are they that mourn; for they shall be comforted. Blessed are the meek; for they shall inherit the earth. Blessed are they that do hunger and thirst after righteousness; for they shall be filled. Blessed are the merciful; for they shall obtain mercy." These are gentle words. How different from the old, iron, brassy clang of the law! "Blessed are the peacemakers; for they shall be called the children of God. Blessed are they who are persecuted for righteousness' sake; for theirs is the kingdom of heaven. Blessed are ye when men shall revile you and persecute you and say all manner of evil against you falsely, for my sake. Rejoice and be exceeding glad; for great is your reward in heaven; for so persecuted they the prophets who were before you."

After this opening, the Sermon goes on with these sharp discriminations between the Old Dispensation and the New, so emphatic and searching: "Ye have heard it said of old, thou shalt not kill; but I of the new say, he that is angry with his brother, hath the kill in his heart. Ye have heard of old, thou shalt love thy neighbor and hate thine enemy; but I say, love thine enemy, and thy persecutor, and thy maligner. Ye have heard of old, thou shalt not commit adultery; but I say the glance of the eye, and the pulse of the heart, are an infraction of my law. When thou doest thine alms, act not as the hypocrites do in the synagogues and in the streets, sounding a trumpet that they may be heard of men. But let not thy left hand know what thy right hand doeth; and thy Father who seeth in secret, shall reward thee openly. When thou prayest, be not like the old prayers at the corners of the streets and in the synagogues, whose chief desire is to be seen and heard of men. But enter into thy closet, and when thou hast shut the door, pray; and thy Father who seeth in secret shall reward thee openly. Judge not, lest ye be judged — and have measured to you that which ye measure to others. Ye have heard of old, an eye for an eye, and a tooth for a tooth; but I say, a cheek for a cheek, and a cloak for a cloak, rather than retaliation in the spirit of revenge. Why beholdest thou the mote that is in thy brother's eye? Thou hypocrite! Cast out the beam from thine own eye, and thou shalt better see the mote in thy neighbor's eye."

By their fruits men are to be known, and not by their professions. "Lord! Lord!" never saves; but a cup of cold water may; and a visit to the sick and imprisoned likewise. He that heareth these sayings of mine and *doeth* them, shall live.

Having preached this Inaugural Sermon, the foundation of his whole Gospel and Dispensation, we behold Christ passing into practical life, doing the work of the Christian; doing what shall stand as the exemplification of what all men are to do, who would be his disciples; works of charity, mercy, instruction, purification; works of reformation; works of redeeming men from the grasp of evil, of lifting them from the sod of degradation to the crown God poises evermore above every man's brow; until finally we come to the end, the *tragic* end, the test end, or finish of a life that knew no blight — no failure.

Thus we perceive a fourfold order of movement. First, a quitting of all wrong in the past; "cease to do evil." Secondly, reconstruction; a going forward, a building up, growing, "learning to do well." Thirdly, "Marvel not that I say unto you, ye must be born again;" inspired, ingrafted, touched, exalted and lifted by grander forces than any in you. We cannot dwell on Regeneration here; it will come up at another time. In the fourth place, you come to the finish of the man, as Christ came to his own finish; that is, maturity without blight; continuing unto the end; making not failure but success, even to the losing of life for the sake of finding it.

Of course, all this was terrible to Jewish ears. It was astonishing, perplexing, bewildering. And I don't wonder; it was entirely natural, and not wrong in all respects. For who were these men? The favored of God; the specialized of all mankind for Divine preference, to whose hands the world were to look for every crumb of comfort and every staff of help. Were not they saved? Had they not the Oracles? Were they not of the Fathers, the consecrated, who received the promise, and who bestowed gifts upon all posterity? Said they, "Have we not, in the great family of God, the rights of primogeniture? Are we not alone the elect?"

Then, look at the expectation of Israel, dreaming of a Messianic reign, of a mighty Comer, a conqueror that should wipe out shame and disaster from memory even, and scepter them with rightful sway over the whole earth. But the reputed Messiah came speaking, not words of royalty, conquest and dominion, but *Repent!* casting aside all pomp and outward glitter as a mere bauble. The boasted glory of nation, the sacredness of altar, the pride of temple and holiness of priest, all went for nothing. This new gospel, ringing out, Repent! continually, as if all the past were only dream, or evil! — trust and confidence were confounded by it.

But not less terrible was it to the Gentile world, filled with pride — pride of learning, philosophy, science, art, and full of license.

Those things, I say, were not wrong always. We don't wonder men were startled. Their idea of religion was far different. With them it was a thing of institutions, of beliefs, of forms and ceremonies. He who kept every jot and tittle of this externality, was the man for God. Hence that sharp discrimination between the Old and the New in the Inaugural Sermon. Ye have heard it said so and so; but *I* say so and so. It was a passage from the dominion of sense to the dominion of spirit; and it seemed sudden, violent, to those locked in the ancient forms. It was a turning away from the mere circumstances of the man, and a fixing directly upon the matter in hand, the man himself. "*Men*, I speak to, and speak of, and for," says this new Teacher. All else is indifferent.

Without doubt, this Dispensation introduced by

John the Baptist and carried on by Jesus Christ, involved the greatest Reformation the world ever knew. It involved radical, immutable principles. Not only was it external in form, but drastically, ultimately internal in fact and essence; not only local and temporal, but universal in its nature and purpose; not only individual, but the scope of it included the whole race. It struck for broad generalities. They could not be developed then, but they were included in the spirit and purpose of the new order. Not only for yesterday and to-day, but for to-morrow and all to-morrows; there was grandeur in the conception and sweep of it. No single act or scene, era or cycle, could play the Divine drama. The plot was all-inclusive as time — as eternity.

The system of transplanting in the world of nature, is a page from her hidden wisdom and an illustration of the early development of the Christian religion. The florist, the pomologist and the agriculturist will tell you that no plant will do so well left to grow just where its seed germinates, as it will if taken up and set out — transplanted. Then it will throw out new fibrous roots, and gather fresh contributions from external and varied sources, and come to growth and perfection. Precisely so with moral and intellectual truths. Christianity had at once to be eradicated from the seed-bed where it first sprouted, and to be transplanted into the Gentile life. It had to be transplanted from the whole Jewish nation and economy, into the great universal Cosmos or world-life, regardless of provincial limitations in any sense. Not until this transplanting do we observe that Christianity began to achieve her victories. She did nothing in Palestine. And Palestine to-day is nothing but the spot where she shook off the dust of her feet. She could display no triumphs there. It is just so with the whole of us who stick to the old beds where our ideas first sprouted, and refuse to be transplanted, or to let in any new ideas, any new forces or contributions to our strength and life.

Christianity could not display herself in the limited cradle of her birth. She must have a broad, boundless theatre on which to act. She cannot display herself now entirely. She is under limitations to-day. She must emancipate herself from the monopoly of the church and get out into the world. Yet there are those who are always seeking to bind her to old restrictions, to churches, customs, notions, confining her to the primitive flower-pots in which she first germinated, throwing up walls and fences around the early gardens where she was first planted. In that way she would perish were she mortal. She must have room; she must be transplanted into broader, newer, higher conditions, out of her native Palestine, into "all the world" of truth and life and man.

There are reform-words breaking through the still air of our life to-day, as startling as any that ever broke the slumbers of old Judaism, falling from lip of herald or Messiah. Gongs of retribution are rending the air all around us — if we only had ears to hear — ominous as any that ever reverberated through the halls of old Athens or Rome or Babylon or Jerusalem. In the religious thinking of to-day, God and his Christ are moving out of the monopolies of Scribes and Pharisees, Sadducees, Soothsayers and Medicinemen, into MAN'S NATURE — into the actual life of the world. Why, pure religion is shaking from her wings the accumulated dust and leaden clogs that have held her fast; and to-day is flying through the air, crying, "Repent! Repent! for the kingdom of heaven is at hand." Bigots and Pharisees will have less leave to hide their sins beneath borrowed cloaks, saying: "We are more righteous than thou." Neither can the children of the world, always wiser than the "children of light," derive any advantage merely from the sagacity which sees through the worn-out and rent garments of mere profession. No boasting for either. For God is breaking down the walls of artificial partitions and distinctions among men; He is tearing off the veils and shibboleths from one party, and scattering the flimsy excuses of the other. He is aiming directly at the *Man* and the *Woman* personally; at the measure of their worth, not their claims. God to-day, as never before, is bidding religion seek the law of man's life and the core of his character; and by these to abide in her final adjudications. This is the work of the New Dispensation broken upon the world by the Baptist's word "Repent," taken up by Christ through the same word, and carried on to this day. And on it will go, broader and higher, conquering and to conquer.

Precisely this, which pealed out like a trumpet-blast eighteen hundred years ago in the ears of ancient bigotry, self-righteousness and sin,—this thundertone of God in the Christ of to-day—it is this that is crashing through the Pantheons of superstition, ignorance and idolatry, and the banqueting halls of corruption, and license and sin everywhere. How clean is your soul, O man of the nineteenth century? How divine is thy life, how pure thy character, O woman who rememberest the Mother of the Sacred One? The washing of regeneration,—is it nothing but a card in the Sorcerer's game? Is the devil of sin to be cast out by a sign? Is the great spiritual drenching of thy life something that leaves thy life and character untouched? The myrrh, the frankincense and the aloes, do they sprinkle and make fragrant thy spirit, O disciple, or are they odors for thy garments alone? Is the sprinkling all outside? Is the glory all fresco and red paint? These are questions of the *New* Dispensation, not of the Old.

Alexander Pope was scoffed at by the self-righteous bigots of his time, because he said: "An honest man is the noblest work of God." But if I had authority to say it, I would stand here and declare, that the time is coming when an HONEST MAN shall be crowned Poet Laureate in the Kingdom of God. A careful thinker said not long ago: "An honest God is the noblest work of man." He startled a few; but a finer, clearer truth, has not lately been uttered. And the time will come when men will be noble and honorable enough themselves, not to reflect in their conceptions any dishonoring attribute of their Maker.

We forget that we make our own gods,—the gods we worship,—if not with our hands, with our dreams and speculations and imaginations. The Scribes and Pharisees once, we remember, "thanked God that they were not like other men." To be sure they were not. But the time will come, when it will be more tolerable for Chorazin and Bethsaida, than for Scribes and Pharisees boasting in that way. Bigotry and self-righteousness pulled down widows' houses and ground the faces of the poor to the earth; and after they had done it, threw stones at Jesus for not tithing anise, mint, and cummin, and for picking corn on Sunday. But the time will come, when even "publicans and harlots shall enter the Kingdom of God" before such accusers.

These are all ideas which were hinted in that first pregnant word, "Repent!" The field of their planting, Christ said, is "the world." This field, so planted, the Christian dispensation is to train, cultivate and develop, until the grand seed shall become the grander harvest. These are the sword-truths that pierce to the dividing asunder of the Old and the New; the outward and the inward; show and substance; creeds and character; profession and practice. Ye have heard of old time, "they make clean the outside of the cup and the platter;" but I say unto you, "he that maketh clean the *inside* of the platter and the cup, is clean every whit."

These are the lamps to guide the workmen of truth and fidelity from the first hammer sound of Repentance, to the last finishing stroke that brings the "fullness of the stature" of the perfect man. Not shadows are we seeking to-day; not old refrains are we to repeat, that were music once in ears no longer quick. We are to take living truth as God in his last words has given it; we are to take principles that are everlasting; we are to take purities that are salt and full of heavenly savor; these we are to take, and work them into human *life* and *character*. We are to be MAN-BUILDERS; not dream-builders, not ceremony-builders, not speculation-builders, simply, but *character-builders* through and through. "Repent," was the first stroke in the work; "Reform," carries it on; and the intelligence and fidelity of spiritual life, able to take up and prosecute the work to the crowning finish, constitute the true discipleship of Christ.

Repent — *Reform* — *Regenerate* — this is the practical trinity of Christian religion; these are the hammer-strokes of her divine workmanship; the stately steps of her triumphant march, as she moves on through humanity, conquering and to conquer.

Shall we keep time?

THE END.

RECENT PUBLICATIONS
OF
CLAXTON, REMSEN & HAFFELFINGER.

FOREGLEAMS AND FORESHADOWS OF IMMORTALITY. By Edmund H. Sears. 12mo. New (and Eleventh) Edition, revised and greatly enlarged. Extra cloth, $1.75.

"The 'Foregleams of Immortality' will stand as a lovely classic in sacred literature, and a beautiful inspiration of pure devotional feeling. . . . The best test of merit of a book is when we feel we have been made better by reading it; and while the one now before us widens the field of intellectual vision, and makes solid and substantial the bridge from time to eternity, it quickens the conscience in its sense of duty, and softens the heart with a tender and more celestial love." — *Christian Inquirer.*

"Dr. Sears has done a valuable service to reflecting minds in the preparation of this volume. . . . Nowhere is the argument for immortality more clearly set forth; nowhere are the Scripture facts, which testify to and affirm it, marshalled in closer array, or arranged with more logical consistency. The clear and beautiful style of the author adds new power to the lesson he has sought to teach, and gives added brightness to the page on which it is written." — *Boston Evening Transcript.*

"The other productions of Mr. Sears have been marked by the loftiest moral beauty, in the purest and most elegant diction; but this is his *chef-d'œuvre* in many respects. . . . We know no religious work of the age adapted to make a deeper, more practical, and more gladdening impression on thoughtful and lofty minds." — *Christian Register.*

"Few books have pleased me so much as 'Foregleams of Immortality.' It is full of beauty and truth. The writer is wise from Swedenborg, and has his own gifts besides. I can scarcely conceive of his writings not impressing many, and deeply. I have lent the book and recommended it in England, where the husks of the old theology interfere much with development and growth. Certainly it is a most beautiful and pungent book." — *Mrs. Elizabeth Barrett Browning, in a letter to an American friend.*

"There is much in the details of the volume which is instructive, and especially as regards the reality and some of the features of the intermediate state. . . . The concluding part of the book is entirely new, being on the 'Symphony of Religions,' and sets forth the imperfect but yet valuable testimony of the various heathen religions to the grand truth of Immortality." — *Chicago Advance.*

"A very interesting volume. The author has herein discussed the pregnant theme of Immortality with signal ability, clothing his thoughts in language so chaste and elegant, and illustrating his ideas by such a profusion of appropriate imagery, that the book has all the fascination of a beautiful poem." — *The Swedenborgian.*

REGENERATION. By Edmund H. Sears. New Edition, revised and enlarged. 12mo. Extra cloth, $1.25.

"A fresh vivid presentation of an important theme — all the more valuable as the utterance of one who has thought deeply and felt profoundly about it. The reader will find in these pages no dry discussion of a hackneyed subject, but familiar truth presented with beauty of diction in a singularly felicitous and impressive manner, and possessing a fascination which will win his attention from the beginning of the book to its close. . . . The three volumes ('Regeneration,' 'Foregleams,' and 'The Heart of Christ,') together are a valuable contribution to religious and theological literature, and one which any man might be proud to have made. As now published, they would form most acceptable additions to the library of any Sunday-School, parish, or clergyman." — *Boston Evening Transcript.*

"Mr. Sears' volume on 'Regeneration' is one of the profoundest and most exhaustive treatises on that subject, extant. The way in which he unfolds the laws of our inner life in the orderly process of spiritual development, will be a revelation to most of those who read it for the first time." — *Arthur's Home Magazine.*

"A work full of the deepest and most nourishing spiritual truths — truths never more needed than they are at the present day and hour. Among devotional works it stands in the front rank; and alike in the sweetness of its spirit and the beauty of its language, it commends itself to every sincere Christian. . . . It is a good book to have by one. Its frequent perusal and study can hardly fail to enrich the spiritual life and lead to a firmer faith and a larger charity." — *The Christian Register.*

"Never, we venture to say, has the subject of regeneration been treated in a manner at once so profound, philosophic, exhaustive, logical, and scriptural, as in this charming volume." — *Boston New Church Magazine.*

THE FOURTH GOSPEL, THE HEART OF CHRIST. By Edmund H. Sears. 12mo. pp. 551. Extra cloth, $2.50.

"The Fourth Gospel, the Heart of Christ, is a book of extraordinary interest; . . . a rich and fresh contribution to the literature of the ages touching the life of our Lord. It is instructive and suggestive in the highest ranges of Christian thought and feeling." — *The Congregationalist.*

"No book of recent American theology is likely to win more notice from thoughtful readers than this handsome volume by Edmund H. Sears, of 551 pages." — *The Church and State.*

"The book of Dr. Edmund H. Sears, entitled 'The Heart of Christ,' is destined, we believe, to exert a powerful influence upon the opinions of thinking men in all branches of the Church." — *New York Independent.*

LETTERS ON THE FUTURE LIFE, addressed to HENRY WARD BEECHER. By B. F. Barrett. 12mo. Extra cloth, $1.00.

CONTENTS.—I. MR. BEECHER'S POSITION CRITICALLY EXAMINED. II. SWEDENBORG'S CLAIM — AND CREDIBILITY. III. HIS PHILOSOPHY OF SPIRIT-SEEING. IV. VINDICATION OF HIS CLAIM — by adducing what he says concerning Death and Resurrection; the Form of Man's Spirit; Light and Heat in Heaven; the Scenery of Heaven; Societies in Heaven; Time and Space in Heaven; Houses in Heaven; Temples and Worship in Heaven; Governments in Heaven; a Heaven for Gentiles; Children in Heaven; the Rich and Poor in Heaven; Marriages in Heaven; Employments in Heaven; the Happiness of Heaven; the Life that leads to Heaven; the Nature of Hell; the Fire of Hell — what it is; Man's Book of Life, &c., &c. V. NEED AND TENDENCY OF HIS DISCLOSURES. VI. COLLATERAL TESTIMONY.

"A small volume with a great deal in it." — *The Golden Age.*

"We believe these Letters will produce a favorable impression upon the candid reader. There is [in them] a vigor and terseness most welcome in these days of long-drawn-out and tedious attempts at generalization." — *Boston New Church Magazine.*

"The literature of Swedenborgianism is growing every year; and what is noticeable about it is its good literary form, its earnest spirit, and the vigor and culture that it shows. . . . Any one fond of such speculation will read this lively little book with interest; for the presentation of the subject is animated and earnest." — *New Haven Palladium.*

"No one of the many works in the same vein — some of which that are singularly able and lucid have been prepared by Mr. Barrett — have more earnestness, practically applied, than this." — *Philadelphia North American.*

"A grand and impressive statement of the New Church doctrine of the Future Life, eminently calculated to enlighten and interest the general reader." — *New Church Independent.*

LETTERS ON THE DIVINE TRINITY, addressed to HENRY WARD BEECHER. By B. F. Barrett. New and enlarged edition. 12mo. Extra cloth, $1.00.

A trenchant but friendly criticism of Mr. Beecher's view of the Trinity, as stated in his sermon on "Understanding God;" and presenting with great clearness and force the New Doctrine on this subject, together with the Scriptural and rational evidence in its support.

PUBLICATIONS OF CLAXTON, REMSEN & HAFFELFINGER.

THE NEW VIEW OF HELL; Showing its Nature, Whereabouts, Duration, and How to Escape it. By B. F. Barrett. 12mo. Extra cloth, $1.00.

CONTENTS.—I. THE NEW DISPENSATION. II. THE OLD DOCTRINE OF HELL. III. THE NEW VIEW. IV. THE SCRIPTURE ARGUMENT—SHEÖL, HADES, GEHENNA, AND THE LAKE OF FIRE. V. HELL, THE CHOSEN HOME OF ALL WHO GO THERE. VI. THE DURATION OF HELL. VII. SOME EVIDENCE OF ITS DURATION—PHILOSOPHICAL AND SCRIPTURAL. VIII. WHY CANNOT THE RULING LOVE BE CHANGED AFTER DEATH? IX. DISPLAYS OF THE DIVINE BENIGNITY IN HELL. X. IS HELL TO UNDERGO ANY CHANGE? IF SO, OF WHAT NATURE? XI. THE DEVIL AND SATAN. XII. PRACTICAL BEARINGS OF THE QUESTION. XIII. HOW TO ESCAPE HELL.

"A succinct and intelligible statement of Swedenborg's doctrine of retribution. It contains . . . much that is profoundly true, and much that is exceedingly suggestive." — *New York Independent.*

"A really valuable contribution to the world's stock of religious ideas. . . . The book, taken as a whole, is of great interest, and we commend it to our readers as worthy of attentive perusal." — *New York Sun.*

"There is not a Christian man or woman in the world, who would not be benefited by the reading of this book." — *Westfield News-Letter.*

"In 'The New View of Hell' is put forth one of the most striking and pregnant of Swedenborg's thoughts — that, too, whose influence on orthodoxy has been most observable — his conception of Hell as a state, not a place, and as such, the chosen home of all who go there." — *New York Evening Mail.*

"The author illustrates and enforces the main idea of his volume with great fulness of detail and frequent beauty of expression. His discussion is conducted with an admirable sweetness of spirit, unusual in theological controversy." — *New York Tribune.*

LECTURES ON THE NEW DISPENSATION, signified by the New Jerusalem of the Apocalypse. By B. F. Barrett. 12mo. Extra cloth, $1.15.

The design of this volume is to unfold and elucidate the leading doctrines taught by Emanuel Swedenborg. And it is considered one of the best works for this purpose ever published. *The London Intellectual Repository* calls it "an admirable work for making one acquainted with the doctrines of the New Church [as taught by Swedenborg]."

www.ingramcontent.com/pod-product-compliance
Lightning Source LLC
Chambersburg PA
CBHW021954220426
43663CB00007B/810